Bookkeeping for Beginners

Learn the Essential Basics of Bookkeeping for Small Businesses with Simple and Effective Methods Step-by-Step: Comprehensive Accounting, Financial Statements, and QuickBooks

Warren Piper Ruell

Please note the information contained within this document is for educational and entertainment purposes only. All effort has been executed to present accurate, up to date, reliable, complete information. No warranties of any kind are declared or implied. Readers acknowledge that the author is not engaging in the rendering of legal, financial, medical or professional advice. The content within this book has been derived from various sources. Please consult a licensed professional before attempting any techniques outlined in this book.

By reading this document, the reader agrees that under no circumstances is the author responsible for any losses, direct or indirect, that are incurred as a result of the use of information contained within this document, including, but not limited to, errors, omissions, or inaccuracies.

Description

This book is a complete introduction to bookkeeping and accounting principles written specifically for the independent business owner.

Entrepreneurship and small business ownership are on the rise. The gig economy has created a huge upsurge in independent contractors, freelancers, and work-form-home professionals. All of this new activity in the business world is exciting, but to really succeed at running your own business, you'll need to know more than just basics of selling quality goods and service.

Starting and operating an independent business can be one of the most exciting and rewarding efforts you ever undertake. An independent business provides you with a platform to share your expertise and knowledge and use your time profitably. But there are also challenges and obstacles to overcome.

If you're like most people, you would probably prefer to spend your time representing your business to customers and clients. After all, it's your passion, and that's why you started a business to begin with, right? Don't let the idea of bookkeeping, paying bills, and learning about accounting principles dampen your enthusiasm. Learning the basics of effective bookkeeping can help you master the fundamentals of managing your business's finances. And that can free you to spend more time doing what you really love. Bookkeeping for Beginners starts with an overview of bookkeeping basics:

- What is bookkeeping?
- Why is bookkeeping important?
- How does bookkeeping work?
- What is the difference between bookkeeping and accounting?

From there, Bookkeeping for Beginners walks readers through the most impotent aspects of effective professional bookkeeping, including:

- Double-entry vs. single-entry bookkeeping.
- How to record debits and credits.
- Cash vs. accrual accounting.
- Recording assets, liabilities, expenses, income, and equity.
- Creating a chart of accounts.
- Creating and understanding financial statements.

- Using financial journals and ledgers.

Next, Bookkeeping for Beginners walks you through two case studies show you step-by-step how to:
- Set up a single-entry cash bookkeeping system.
- Set up a double-entry accrual bookkeeping system.
- Close the books and generate financial statements.

Finally, Bookkeeping for Beginners brings it all back home by covering the latest in technology and business innovation:
- Guidance on how to run a business.
- Using QuickBooks to automate bookkeeping and accounting.
- Adapting bookkeeping methods to meet the needs of your business.

Whether you are just starting out as a business owner or looking for the extra insight to make your existing business the profitable and enjoyable venture you know it can be, Bookkeeping for Beginners will set you on the track to success!

Table of Contents

Chapter 1: Bookkeeping Basics

What is Bookkeeping?

Figure 1: Free Image

According to the *Dictionary of Business*, bookkeeping is defined simply as "the keeping of the financial records of a business or an organization." This is a fairly straightforward definition and seems obvious, but it doesn't reveal much to anyone interested in learning about how bookkeeping for small businesses works or why it is important. So, a more detailed definition will help to introduce all the topics that will be discussed throughout this book. The basic function of any bookkeeper is to record all the financial transactions that occur throughout each business day of any business. There are two important points here.

The first point is that the function of the bookkeeper is to record financial transactions – that's it. Bookkeeping does not involve analyzing the financial data to ensure compliance with tax laws, or to conduct audits, or any other complex forms of complex methods of assessing financial data. The more complex aspects of analyzing financial records and producing financial statements is the job of the accountant. Although this book will touch on some of those aspects, its main focus will be on the responsibilities of the bookkeeper. Bookkeeping is quite simply the job of ensuring that all the money that flows into and out of a business's financial accounts is recorded accurately and according to an established and organized system.

The second point is that because the primary focus of bookkeeping is ensuring that all financial transactions are recorded accurately, effective bookkeeping requires at least a basic understanding of established bookkeeping methods and which system is best for any given business. Bookkeeping systems may use one of two types of "entry systems" – single-entry and double-entry. They may also use one of two types of accounting methods – cash-based or accrual-based. We will examine the difference in greater detail later, but for now, suffice it to say that single-entry systems are best for very small businesses, while double-entry systems are more suitable for larger businesses.

Why Is Bookkeeping Important?

In this age of digital computing and the internet, many people have made the assumption that bookkeeping is obsolete. After all, the term "bookkeeping" is derived from the practice of writing down financial transactions by hand into paper ledgers or books with pages specifically designed to keep track of these types of records.

Now that the internet has spawned online banking, e-payment apps, and digital currency, many people have mistakenly assumed that these concerns are no longer relevant. But assuming that you can arrive at an accurate assessment of your business's financial condition by simply checking the balances in your business checking account online is a huge mistake. Although it is true that you can depend on the bank to maintain accurate records of deposits, withdrawals, and current balances in your bank accounts, these records are not the same as the daily transaction records of your business. The proliferation of spreadsheet software like Excel, as well as small business bookkeeping software like QuickBooks, is definitely an exciting development for all small business owners and entrepreneurs. These tools can open up the door to faster growth, greater productivity, and a more efficient and enjoyable business operation. But these tools do not replace the fundamental requirement of all businesses to maintain accurate records of their financial transactions.

Effective bookkeeping can help entrepreneurs and business owners in a variety of ways, regardless of the type or size of the business they are running. Here are some of the ways your business can benefit from an effective system of bookkeeping:

- Bookkeeping ensures your personal finances will be kept separate from your business finances.
- Bookkeeping allows you to detect and correct banking, billing, and accounting errors.

- Bookkeeping allows you to optimize your business for maximum efficiency and profitability.
- Bookkeeping helps you understand where your business fits in with your overall plan for growth.
- Bookkeeping can help you qualify for tax deductions.
- Bookkeeping can help you establish better business credit and qualify for loans.

How Does Bookkeeping Work?

An effective system of bookkeeping must consider several necessary functions of your business' financial functions. Traditionally, these concerns could be addressed universally by using any standardized ledger that allowed for tracking all the daily expenses involved in running your business, as well as all of the income resulting from successful transactions. As technology has evolved, so have bookkeeping methods. There are many bookkeeping software programs available as online services run by bookkeeping companies, as well as programs and spreadsheets that can be downloaded to your computer to allow you to complete the basic data entry and transaction recording necessary to keep your company's finances straight.

Although much of the software may make it easier to manage many of the tasks involved in bookkeeping, bookkeeping itself still requires accuracy, diligence, and attention to detail. As the computer programming slogan says, "Garbage in, garbage out." So it is with bookkeeping. Finding the right system for your business – whether you choose a more traditional paper-based system, an entirely electronic system, or some combination of both – you will need to track all the transactions that occur within your business every day. The more effective your system of bookkeeping, the easier it will be for you to check for errors, ensure consistency and accuracy, and ultimately increase profitability and accountability.

Basic Accounting Principles

As we discussed earlier, there are two major types of entry systems: single-entry accounting and double-entry accounting. With single-entry accounting systems, all transactions – whether for financial resources that are coming into the business, or for financial resources that are flowing out of the business – are entered only once. Thus, when you receive payment for a sale, you record the transaction once as income; when you write a check to pay a bill, you record the transaction once, as an expense.

With a double entry-system, every transaction is recorded twice. In the example above, when you receive a payment for sale, you record the income as a credit, but you also debt your inventory for an equal value – the cost of the item or service you provided. In the second example, when you pay write a check to pay a bill, you may debt the business checking account for the amount of the expense, but you will also credit your monthly expense account for the same amount. Double-entry systems are more complex but also more reliable and flexible and can accommodate more growth over time.

There are also two basic accounting methods, and every bookkeeping system will use either one or the other. The two systems are cash-based accounting and accrual-based accounting.

With cash-based accounting, transactions are only recorded when the transactions actually occur. Thus, if you have bills to pay before the end of the month, you will not include them as expenses in a cash-based system until the money actually leaves the business checking account. Similarly, if you have made ten sales, you cannot count them as income until you actually receive payment from your customers.

With accrual-based accounting, you may record bills and invoices as liabilities and assets, whether or not you have paid the bills or received payment for the sales. In this system, bills that still have to be paid are called "accounts payable," and invoices that have not yet been paid are called "accounts receivable." The accrual-based system allows you to create reports that indicate projected income and projected expenses, as well as actual income and actual expenses.

Introduction to Bookkeeping and Accounting

Many people use the terms "bookkeeping" and "accounting" interchangeably. Although these two practices are related, there are several fundamental differences between them. Essentially, the difference is that the bookkeeper is responsible for recording every single transaction conducted by a business and classifying according to whether it is an expense or a form of income, as well as what type of expense and what type of income. The accountant is responsible for taking all the information about transactions compiled by the bookkeeper, analyzing that information to prepare office financial reports and statements, and making recommendations based on interpretations of the company's financial condition.

In one sense, the account's focus is narrower than that of the bookkeeper. In addition, although bookkeepers may obtain certification as a professional, their expertise is likely to come from on-the-job training and experience. Accountants, on the other hand, generally must obtain a degree in accounting and be licensed as Certified Public Accountants before they can work in any professional environment. In the hierarchy of the corporate structure, the accountant ranks higher than the bookkeeper. Although the bookkeeper may have broader knowledge and experience of bookkeeping systems, the accountant's specialized training qualifies him for more technical and complex assignments.

The following is a list of responsibilities commonly assigned to bookkeepers:

- issuing invoices to customers for goods and services sold
- receiving and documenting incoming invoices from suppliers for inventory and supplies purchased
- documenting cash, credit, and other forms of payment received from customers
- issuing payments to suppliers
- documenting changes in inventory levels
- managing payroll records
- receding and documenting petty cash transactions

By contrast, an accountant may be responsible for any of the following responsibilities:

- creating a chart of all accounts
- setting up the general ledger that will be used by the bookkeeper
- designing financial statements
- creating customized financial reports
- adjusting transaction records to ensure compliance with accounting standards
- creating budgets and comparing actual performance to benchmarks
- preparing and filing tax returns based on bookkeeping records
- creating a system of accountability
- designing record-keeping systems

Chapter 2: Bookkeeping

Principles and Fundamental

Differences

Figure 2: Free Image

If you're like most people, you probably think of the words "debit" and "credit" in terms of the kind of card you use to pay for items when you go shopping. When you use your debit card, the money comes directly out of your checking account; but when you use your credit card, instead of money being deducted from your bank account, the amount of the purchase is added to the total bill you will pay your credit card company at the end of the month.

This is a very basic understanding of debits and credits can help you navigate the terminology of this part of recording financial transactions for your business. However, in the world of bookkeeping, this essential concept is somewhat more complex.

First, before we explore the specifics of how debits and credits are used to record transactions in bookkeeping, let's consider the basic equation upon which all accounting is based:

$$\text{Assets} = \text{Liabilities} + \text{Equity}$$

Whenever you see a mathematical equation, you know that the two elements on either side of the equals sign must have the same numeric value, so the following two equations are correct:

$$2 + 1 + 1 = 4$$
$$3 + 1 = 4$$

But this equation is incorrect:

$$2 + 3 = 4$$

Because the value of a business is calculated using the accounting equation, Assets = Liabilities + Equity, the numeric values of these terms must be a balanced equation. If they are not, then your business's books are out of balance, and in order to create accurate financial statements, you will have to locate where you have made bookkeeping errors.

Next, before we examine debits and credits in detail, we should take a moment to understand the terms in the accounting equation.

- Assets are any resources that your company owns that represent a future value and can be expressed in monetary value. Cash is one type of asset, but there are many others. For example, investments, inventory, real estate, office supplies, equipment, and accounts receivable, all represent resources that you own and that can be assigned a monetary value. In addition, so-called "intangible assets" include your company's reputation, your client base, the perceived value of your brand, etc.
- Liabilities are the amount of outstanding financial obligations owed by your company. So, your company's liabilities may include the remaining balance on any mortgages, equipment leases, or business loans; accounts payable; or amounts received for future sales that have not yet been delivered.

- Equity is the amount of financial interest all of a company's shareholders have in the company. For example, if you buy 1,000 shares of stock in a new startup company at $2.25 per share, you can personally claim $2,250.00 of that company's value as yours.

So, the accounting equation, Assets = Liabilities + Equity, means that in order for your company's books to be considered balanced and in order, you must be able to show that the total value of all of your assets is exactly equal to the total value of all your liabilities plus the total value of all of the equity all shareholders may have in your company.
This seems like a daunting task, and that's why accounting uses both debits and credits to record transactions.

Importance of Debit and Credit Accounting

We began this chapter by considering a common understanding of debits and credits – using your debit card takes money out of your checking account; using a credit card adds money to your credit card bill. This is a great start to understanding the importance of using debits and credits to keep accurate books, but in terms of bookkeeping, this concept is more complex.

First, consider the definition of assets above. There are many types of assets, ranging from the balance in your business's main checking account, to the total value of your inventory, to the value of your supplies and equipment, to the value of all the sales you have made for which you are awaiting payment. As a result, an accurate bookkeeping system will need more than just one account to track assets.

Next, you may also have many types of liabilities, including accounts payable and future sales, so you may have more than one account to record all your liabilities.

Finally, in addition to assets, liabilities, and equity, your bookkeeping system will have to keep track of revenue, expenses, gains, and losses.

Taken together, these categories of financial accounts – assets, liabilities, equity, revenue, expenses, gains, and losses – comprise what accountants call the chart of accounts and depending on the size and complexity of your company, the chart of accounts can become fairly complicated.

One more step, and the importance of debits and credits will become clear. Returning to the original example of shopping at your local department store, consider what happens when you buy something with your debit card – the amount of money in your checking account is reduced, but the amount of money in the department store's checking account is increased. In addition, although you have less cash after making the purchase with the debit card, you have increased the value of your assets by the value of the term you purchased; and in return, the value of the store's inventory has decreased by the value of the time they sold. The difference in making the purchase with a credit card is that instead of decreasing the amount of money in your checking account, you increase the amount of money you owe; similarly, the store does not receive an increase in the amount of money in their checking account, but they do see an increase in the value of their accounts receivable.

Thus, the concept behind debits and credits is that every single transaction has two parts – money is taken from one account, and money is added to another account. Because a company's books account for a potentially complex chart of accounts, a system of debits and credits allows the bookkeeper to record all transactions accurately and consistently.

Recording Debit and Credit in an Account

Figure 3: Free Image

First, remember that in accounting, debit is abbreviated dr. and credit is abbreviated cr. Second, although it is common to associate debit with deducting money and credit with adding money, debits and credits in bookkeeping are used differently. Depending on which type of transaction the company engages in and which type of account is affected, debits and credits may either increase or decrease the value of any given account. Specifically:

- For asset accounts (e.g., your company's checking account):
    - A debit will increase the value of the account; a credit will decrease the value of the account.
- For liability accounts (e.g., your accounts payable account):
    - A debit will decrease the value of the account; a credit will increase the value of the account.
- For equity accounts (e.g., the shares an investor holds in your company):
    - A debit will decrease the value of the account; a credit will increase the value of the account.

This seems to be the reverse order of the way you may normally think of debits and credits because it is based on the accounting equation, Assets = Liabilities + Equity. Thus, you cannot increase your assets unless you also increase your liabilities or equity. As a result, debits and credits within a bookkeeping system function differently than in a simple check register.

Of course, in some cases, recording a balanced transaction may require increasing the value of one asset account while decreasing the value of another asset account (instead of a liability or equity account). In these cases, there are additional rules that govern the function of debits and credits:

- For revenue accounts:
  - A debit decreases the balance and a credit increases the balance.
- For expense accounts:
  - A debit will increase the balance and a credit will decrease the balance.
- For gain accounts:
  - A debit decreases the balance and a credit increases the balance.
- For loss accounts:
  - A debit will increase the balance and a credit will decrease the balance.

Regardless, in terms of an actual book of accounts, debits are transaction values that are entered on the left side of an account, and credits are transaction values that are entered on the right side of an account.

Third, for every single transaction in bookkeeping, the total amount recorded as a debit must be offset by the exact same amount recorded as credit. If the two sides of the transaction are unequal, the books will not balance, and the bookkeeping system will not accept the entry.

Let's look at some specific examples to clarify the concepts above.

For the first example, let's assume your company sells computer accessories. One of your customers purchases a video camera attachment for a laptop computer at a cost of $375.00. The sale results in an increase in the value of your cash account. It also means that you have increased your revenue by converting inventory into cash. To record this transaction using debits and credits, the bookkeeper will use two accounts: cash and revenue. When you sold the camera attachment to the customer, you received $375.00 in cash, so the cash account is debited for 375. To record the associated increase in revenue, the bookkeeper credits the revenue account for the same amount – 375.

Account	Debit	Credit

Cash	375	
Revenue		375

Alternatively, the records may be displayed as follows:

Cash	
Debits	Credits
375	

Revenue	
Debits	Credits
	375

In the next example, let's assume that your company needs 10 new servers, and each server costs $1,000. You don't want to use your cash account to make this purchase, so you instruct your purchasing agent to buy them on credit. The purchase results in an increase to the value of your fixed assets account. Because they were purchased on credit, there will be an equal increase to the value of your accounts payable. Here is how the bookkeeper will record the transaction:

Account	Debit	Credit
Fixed Assets	10,000	
Accounts Payable		10,000

Again, the same relationship can be displayed as follows:

Fixed Assets	
Debits	Credits
375	

Accounts Payable

Debits	Credits
	375

Finally, here are some additional guidelines to help get you oriented to the world of debits and credits:

1. Debit-Credit Table

Account Type	Increase	Decrease
Assets	Debit	Credit
Expenses	Debit	Credit
Liabilities	Credit	Debit
Equity	Credit	Debit
Revenue	Credit	Debit

2. Debit-Credit Acronyms

The following types of accounts (DEAL) are increased with a debit:

- **D**ividends
- **E**xpenses
- **A**ssets
- **L**osses

The following types of accounts (GIRLS) are increased with a credit:

- **G**ains
- **I**ncome
- **R**evenues
- **L**iabilities
- **S**tockholders' Equity

3. Debit-Credit Rules

Recording a debit means:

- Increasing the value of an asset account
- Increasing the value of an expense account
- Decreasing the value of a liability account
- Decreasing the value of an equity account
- Decreasing the value of revenue
- Debits are always recorded on the left

Recording a credit means:

- Decreasing the value of an asset account
- Decreasing the value of an expense account
- Increasing the value of a liability account
- Increasing the value of an equity account
- Increasing the value of revenue
- Credit are always recorded on the right

The Accrual Method of Bookkeeping

Now that you have a basic understanding of debits and credits and how they are used to record transactions, we will discuss the accrual method of bookkeeping. When a bookkeeper uses accrual-based accounting, he or she will record all transactions based on when the transaction occurs, rather than when money changes hands. For example, if you make a sale in January, but you don't expect the invoice to be paid until March, a bookkeeper using the accrual method will record the sale in January rather than waiting until the invoice is paid. Similarly, if you sell goods or services to a client on credit, the accrual method of bookkeeping allows you to claim the entire sale at the time the transaction takes place, rather than recording partial sale every time an installment payment is received. Accounting for purchases and expenses using the accrual method is similar – for purchases made on credit, the entire expense, not just the amount of money that changes hands – is recorded at the time of the transaction.

Differences between the Accrual Method and the Cash Method

The cash-based method of bookkeeping is based on cash flow rather than credit and accounts receivable. When a bookkeeper uses the cash-based method, he will only record transactions when cash is paid or received. Thus, if you make a sale, deliver the goods, and send an invoice to your customer in January, but your customer does not send you a check until March, the bookkeeper will record the sale in March, when the payment is received, not in January, when the sale was made. Similarly, if you incur expenses to deliver goods or services to a customer, a bookkeeper using a cash-based method will record the expenses at the time you pay for them, rather than making them part of the entire cost of the sale in the invoice to the customer. For example, if you have to travel to another town to access confidential files as part of generating a professional report, the accrual-based method would allow the bookkeeper to defer recording the cost of those expenses until the invoice is generated; using the cash-based method, the daily expenses of any contract will be recorded as they are incurred and paid by the employee.

The essential difference between these two methods is that the accrual-based method can allow your bookkeeper to create a more accurate picture of your overall income and expenses; as a result, it is a better method for business owners concerned about monitoring their profitability. On the other hand, the strength of the cash-based method of bookkeeping is that you will have a better picture of your daily cash flow.

You will have to identify which type of bookkeeping method you use when you file your taxes, and if you change the method, you will have to notify the Internal Revenue Service by filing a Form 3115, Change in Accounting Method. In addition, if you use an accrual-based method of accounting, you have to use the double-entry method of bookkeeping. We examined the double-entry method, which uses debits and credits, above. The next two sections discuss the differences between double-entry accounting and single-entry accounting.

Single-Entry Bookkeeping (Advantages and Disadvantages)

Single-entry bookkeeping can be compared to keeping track of transaction in your check register. Bookkeeping methods that use the single-entry method only require the bookkeeper to record transactions as they are made, usually bills that are paid from or deposits that are placed into the company's main checking account. This fairly simple form of bookkeeping is appropriate for small companies that do not engage in many transactions. The following is an example of a transaction record using the single-entry method:

Cash Account				
Date	Transaction	Debit	Credit	Balance
January 1, 2020	Balance forward			$100,000.00
January 5, 2020	Payment received	$2,500.00		$102,500.00
January 7, 2020	Rent paid		$750.00	$101,750.00

Date	Description	Debit	Credit	Balance
January 10, 2020	Payroll processed		$40,000.00	$61,750.00
January 12, 2020	Cash sale	$8,000.00		$69,750.00
January 15, 2020	Payment received	$5,500.00		$75,250.00
January 17, 2020	Equipment purchased		$2,000.00	$73,250.00
January 20, 2020	Cash sale	$5,000.00		$78,250.00
January 25, 2020	Utilities paid		$450.00	$77,800.00
January 30, 2020	Payment received	$2,000.00		$79,800.00

Clearly, the advantage with single-entry bookkeeping is the simplicity of the system. A short learning curve and the immediate accessibility and transferability of this kind of bookkeeping from your experiences in personal finance to business bookkeeping makes it an attractive option. However, if your business has any degree of complexity, or if you require a more accurate method of tracking your expenses, single-entry bookkeeping may not address your needs.

Double-Entry Method (Advantages and Disadvantages)

We discussed the double-entry method in the section above entitled, "Recording Debit and Credit in an Account." This type of accounting is obviously more complex that single-entry bookkeeping, However, as we have discussed, only the double-entry method will allow you to record complex transactions that involve more than one type of account. In addition, double-entry accounting can allow you to create a more accurate picture of your company's overall financial condition, including current profitability and cost efficiency. These models can be used to generate reports and make predictions for future growth, secure funding, and identify opportunities for tax breaks or optimization.

Differences Between Excel and Other

Software

The system of debits and credits that is used throughout all accounting systems in the contemporary global environment was developed by a Franciscan monk long before even the electric calculator was invented, let alone the mainframe computer, the digital phone, or virtual bookkeeping spreadsheets, apps, and services.

Traditionally, even the most complex accounting and bookkeeping systems were all maintained by entering transactions by hand into paper ledgers. Some argue that the discipline required to maintain paper ledgers and account journals translates into greater fiscal awareness and better business development and policy making decisions. There is much truth to these sentiments; however, it is not reasonable to expect everyone to return to keeping paper-based records of the company's transactions. Regardless, it is important to consider the purpose and the nature of bookkeeping when you are deciding on the tools and methods to use to keep track of your company's finances.

Microsoft Excel spreadsheets are very versatile and can be adapted to a wide variety of uses. The section on Single-Entry Bookkeeping was created using an Excel spreadsheet. Considering that bookkeeping and accounting had existed primarily as a paper-based practice for most of time, it is possible to adapt Excel spreadsheets for any type of bookkeeping system – single-entry; double-entry; cash-based; or accrual-based. However, a more appropriate use of Excel spreadsheets is to assist the bookkeeper in maintaining accurate paper-based documents. In such cases, most bookkeepers in these cases would likely be utilizing a single-entry cash-based system.

Bookkeeping software has reached a high stage of development, so that many of the functions discussed in this chapter – balancing double-entry transactions and creating reports in accrual-based systems, for example – have been automated. However, simply because the functions themselves have been automated does not mean that the software will do the accounting for you. If you enter the debits and credits of a transaction in a double-entry system incorrectly, the software may refuse to accept the entry or otherwise alert you to the error, but it is still the bookkeeper's responsibility to ensure the accuracy of all financial information entered into the program. Garbage in; garbage out – any accounting or bookkeeping software you use is only as good as the accuracy and completeness of the transaction information you enter into it.

Chapter 3: Assets, Liabilities, and

Capital

Chapter 2 discussed how a system of bookkeeping for a
company with any degree of complexity will use a chart of
accounts (COA) to enable the accurate double-entry of
transactions using debits and credits. Chapter 2 also identified
the main types of account categories these bookkeeping
systems use. In this chapter, we will look at many of the
different types of accounts a company may list in its COA. In
the first part of this chapter, we will identify the main
standardized categories of accounts. The second part of the
chapter will give examples of all the many types of accounts
that can be included under each of the five main account types.

Figure 4: Free Image

Account Categories

Regardless of the size of your company or the type of business services or goods you offer, all the accounts in your COA should fall under one of the five main categories of account types:

- Assets
- Expenses
- Liabilities
- Equity
- Revenue and/or Income

We will also briefly discuss a sixth possible account category:

- Contra-account

General Account Categories

Let's begin by briefly defining and describing the main accounting categories:

Assets

Anything that your company owns that has value can be considered an asset. Assets can be "tangible," i.e., actual, real property such as cash; machinery and equipment; inventory; land; and buildings. Assets can also be "intangible," i.e., things that may have value but that are not actual products or physical objects, such as trademarks; a client base; or a reputation for excellence.

Expenses

Expenses are all the costs associated with running your business. Depending on the complexity and size of your business, you may have many types of expenses. For example, a small business will have to spend money on office supplies, postage, rent, and utilities. Larger businesses will likely have these expenses, but they may also have to spend money on payroll administration, workers' compensation insurance, and travel.

Liabilities

In a sense, liabilities are the opposite of assets. Your liability accounts will list all the money your company owes. There may be many reasons your company owes money. For example, taxes on your payroll account; money you owe to other businesses for equipment purchases; and business loans at your local bank all represent fixed sums that you must pay to outside parties.

Revenue or Income

These accounts represent the amount of money your business earns from selling products or services to customers. Income accounts usually refer to money your company earns from investments, such as interest-bearing accounts with banks or other investment accounts.

Equity

All of your equity accounts represent the amount of money invested in your business or retained as revenue kept as an asset. Recall the basic accounting equation, Assets = Liabilities + Equity. Using a little basic math, we can solve this equation for Equity as follows: Assets - Liabilities = Equity. So, if you total up the value of your assets and subtract everything you owe, what's left is your Equity; this figure tells you how much your company is worth. Depending on the type of business you have, your equity accounts may range from retained earnings to common stock.

Contra-accounts

Not everyone uses contra-accounts. They are created as an accounting tool to offset discrepancies in the rest of your accounts. For example, you may have an account for bad debt allowance, so that if any of your customers fails to pay one of your accounts receivable, you will have a place to record the transaction.

Specific Account Types

Within each account category, any given company may have a wide variety of differing accounts. As you are setting up your COA, it is important to consider all of the types of assets, liabilities, expenses, revenue and equity your company currently has, and what you reasonably expect to encounter as your business grows. A bookkeeping account should be created for each of these concerns, and you will have to decide under which category each of the accounts should be placed.
To help you gain an understanding of how a COA should be structured, this section begins with examples of the many types of accounts that may be included within each of the categories above, and then provides a sample COA. Let's begin by looking at the many types of account you may place under each of the account categories.

Asset Accounts

It's easy enough to understand that assets are things that have value that your company owns. But you can't just total up everything you own, then place the amount in one huge asset account. Even your company's cash reserves will have to separate into different accounts – main checking account (cash) and petty cash, with retained earnings placed in a revenue account. The reason for this specificity is to allow for more control over your company's finances. For example, you will pay all your monthly bills and routine expenses out of your cash account, but you should also fund a petty cash account, so employees have access to funds for unexpected per diem accounts and unplanned purchases. The following is a list of some of the types of accounts commonly listed under Assets:

- Cash: There may be serval cash accounts or only one, depending on the structure of your company. If you have more than one account into which you make deposits or withdraw money for purchase, each of them should be identified:
  - Petty cash
  - Business Checking
  - Business Savings
- Accounts receivable. Total amount of all unpaid invoices sent to customers for goods and

services sold. This account is separate from cash because you have not received the money yet.

- Inventory. The total value of all items your company currently possesses, and that you intend to sell.

- Equipment. The total value of all business equipment that you have purchased and own outright.

- Buildings. The total value of any buildings your company owns.

- Land. The total value of all undeveloped land your company owns.

- Investments. The total value of all securities investments your company owns.

- Prepaid expenses. If your company prepays expenses such as rent or insurance, you may create an account to keep track of the value:
  - Prepaid rent
  - Prepaid insurance

- Supplies. This may be included as part of the equipment account, or you may create a separate account, depending on the nature and complexity of your business.

Expense Accounts

As discussed above, all accounts under the Expenses category should relate to costs associated with producing goods or services, or otherwise with the day-to-day administration of your business. Because accurate bookkeeping requires that you record every single transaction, no matter how small, creating accurate expense accounts is a must. Following are some examples of the types of Expense accounts many businesses may use:

- Cost of Goods Sold (COGS): If you manufacture the goods you sell, you will incur the expenses related to purchasing the material to produce them. Alternatively, you may purchase the items at wholesale and sell them at retail; in this case, the COGS is the amount you pay for the inventory you sell.

- Supplies. If your company produces goods and services, the cost of all supplies required for those purposes should be recorded here.

- Utilities. The monthly cost of electricity, gas, water, and other utility bills should be recorded here.

- Payroll. You may have many different accounts under the payroll heading, depending on the size and complexity of your company.

- Rent. If your company rent retail or office space, you can record transactions here.

- Insurance. Depending on what type of business you operate and insurance regulations, there may be several types of insurance premiums you may have to pay. Record those transactions here.

- Equipment. If your company leases equipment, you can record payments here.

- Advertising. Any expenses associated with marketing and advertising should be recorded here.

- Fees. Increasingly, banks and other institutions may charge fees for their essential services. These are expenses that are separate from the service you are paying for, so you should record them in a separate account.

Liability Accounts

Liabilities are different from expenses. Think of expenses as the monthly or daily costs associated with running your business. Liabilities represent a fixed amount of money that you owe to outside third parties. Generally, you assume liabilities as part of the overall investment for starting and/or growing your business. The following are some examples of the type of Liability accounts many businesses will record in their ledgers:

- Accounts payable. All outstanding financial obligations that the company has not yet paid.
- Sales tax payable. Especially if you sell goods and services online, your company may be required to keep track of the sales tax you owe and pay the IRS annually or quarterly. This account will help you record these transactions.
- Salaries payable. Prior to distributing payroll checks to your employees, the hours they work will accumulate total amounts payable in this account.
- Retirement contributions payable. If your company provides employees with retirement accounts with matching contributions, you can record transactions here.

- Mortgage payable. If you have bought a building for your business and you still owe money on the mortgage, you should record all associated transactions here.
- Taxes payable. Your business may be responsible for a variety of tax obligations, and separate accounts can be set up for each of them:
  - Federal unemployment tax payable.
  - Federal income tax payable.
  - State unemployment tax payable.
  - State income tax payable.
  - Social security tax payable.
- Interest payable. If you have taken out any business loans, you can record amortized interest payable here.

Revenue or Income Accounts

Your business's revenue is the money you earn by providing the goods and services you produce. These accounts track the money you bring as a result of successful business transactions. Typical revenue accounts include:

- Service revenue. If your company provides services, such as accounting, legal services, photography, or plumbing, you should use this account to record each payment received from a customer every time you perform a service.

- Sales revenue. If your business primarily sells products, use this account to record the total value of all receipts for goods sold.
- Interest earned. If your company keeps cash in any interest-bearing bank or investment accounts, you can record payment here.
- Dividends earned. Similar to the interest earned account, all payments received from securities investments that pay shareholders dividends should be recorded here.

Equity Accounts

Equity accounts are used to record all transactions related to money invested in the business. This section of your COA will vary in complexity depending on the type of business you have. Examples of Equity accounts include:

- Capital. This type of equity account is used by small businesses – sole proprietorships and limited partnerships – to record the amount of money the owner has invested in the business.
- Withdrawal. Also used by sole-proprietors or limited partnerships, this type of account

is used to record money taken out of the business for the personal use of the owner.

- Common Stock. Corporations use a common stock account to record the transactions of shareholders who purchase stock in the company.
- Retained Earnings. The counterpart to the Withdrawal account for smaller businesses, this account records transactions related to the payments of dividends or other earnings distributions to owners and shareholders.

Contra-accounts

All the account types above may involve transactions that involve discrepancies, or for which there may not be any specific account set up. In order to ensure your books balance, Contra-Accounts provide a method of rectifying accounting discrepancies. Some examples include:

- Accumulated depreciation. The value of your equipment in assets may decline as a result of depreciation. You can record those values here.
- Bad debt allowance. Your Accounts Receivable account lists all the money your customers owe you for goods sold or services provided.

Sometimes, your customers may default on the invoice. You can record the value of unpaid invoices here.

Sample Chart of Accounts

Below is a sample of how your company's COA may be structured. Notice that a range of numbers is assigned to the accounts within each category. By allowing for larger gaps between the ranges of numbers, you will be able to accommodate any unforeseen changes or growth to your company's business structure.

ABC Goods and Services, Inc.	
Chart of Accounts	
Asset Accounts	
	100 Checking
	101 Petty Cash
	102 Savings
	105 Accounts Receivable
	110 Inventory

111 Equipment
125 Buildings and land

Expense Accounts

200 Cost of Goods Sold
205 Payroll
207 Utilities
210 Rent
215 insurance
220 Equipment leases
230 Fees

Liability Accounts

300 Accounts payable
301 Taxes payable
305 Salaries payable

320 Mortgage payable	
330 Taxes payable	
350 Interest payable	

Revenue Accounts

400 Sales revenue	
500 Service Revenue	
600 Interest Earned	
650 Dividends earned	

Equity Accounts

700 Capital Invested	
750 Withdrawals	

Contra Accounts

800 Depreciation	
900 Bad debts	

Chapter 4: Financial Statements

Throughout the year, the bookkeeper will record and categorize every single transaction in which a company engages, with each transaction placed in the appropriate account. If all these bookkeeping entries are accurate, the books will balance at the end of the year. This information allows the business owner to effectively monitor his or her company's operations and look for ways to improve efficiency, save money, or make new investments. Equally important, well-kept books allow the business owner to produce financial statements that comply with Generally Accepted Accounting Principles (GAAP).

Figure 5: Free Image

What is a Financial Statement?

So, what are these financial statements, and why are they so important? Briefly, financial statements are written records of a company's business and financial activity over the course of previous year designed to convey information about the company's financial performance to shareholders, prospective investors, or regulatory agencies. Accountants prepare financial statements using the information recorded by bookkeepers. All financial statements must comply with GAAP-based formatting and content standards. In many cases, financial statements are audited by private accounting firms or government agencies prior to their release to ensure the information is accurate and reliable.

All financial statements include three major sections:

- Balance sheet
- Income statement
- Cash flow statement

The following sections discuss the uses of financial statements, as well as a detailed examination of each part of a financial statement.

Who Reads Financial Statements?

Financial statements are released to a wide variety of audiences for many different reasons. Possible recipients of financial statements may include:

- Shareholders who want to review the financial statement to evaluate their current investment in a company.
- Investors who are considering investing in a company and want to examine the company's financial performance.
- Brokers, market analysts, and financial advisers who are responsible for recommending investments to their clients.
- Creditors who have to make a decision about whether to lend money to a business.
- Financial regulators and auditors who are hired to investigate a company's financial activity.

Regardless of who is reading the financial statements, the information they convey may serve a variety of purposes, such as:

- The ability of a company to generate cash.
- The ability of a company to pay its debts.
- The overall profitability of a company wand whether it has optimized the use of its resources.
- To determine the soundness of a company's financial structure and its underlying business operations.
- To investigate any of the business's transactions to ensure there are no deviations for GAAP-based standards, legal requirements, or other regulations.

Balance Sheets

The first part of a GAAP-compliant financial statement is the balance sheet. The information included in a balance sheet is designed to provide an overview of a company's assets, liabilities, and equity. Remember again that the basic accounting equation is Assets = Liabilities + Equity. The balance sheet provides a breakdown of these three financial considerations. The main purpose of the balance sheet is to identify how assets are funded – with liabilities like debt, or with equity like capital invested or retained earnings. Generally, a balance sheet will list assets in order of liquidity and liabilities in the order in which they are expected to be paid. Many balance sheets will reflect the format of the basic accounting equation: assets will be listed on the left; liabilities and equity will be listed on the right. Alternatively, assets may be listed at the top, followed by liabilities, and then equity.

One of the most important aspects of the balance sheet to remember is that the information about the company's financial condition it conveys represents only "a snapshot in time." That is, the information about a company's assets, liabilities, and equity as conveyed in a balance sheet is true only for the period of time at which the balance sheet was prepared. So, if the end of the fiscal year is December, and the date of the balance sheet is December 31, the information contained in the balance sheet is true for December 31 of that year only. Though drastic changes are unlikely to occur in the near future, the balance sheet does not convey the company's financial condition over the entire previous year for which the report was created.

The following is an example of a balance sheet:

[Company Name]

Balance Sheet
Date:

Assets	2014	2013
Current Assets		
Cash	11,674	
Accounts receivable		
Inventory		
Prepaid expenses		
Short-term investments		
Total current assets	11,874	-
Fixed (Long-Term) Assets		
Long-term investments	1,208	
Property, plant, and equipment	15,340	
(Less accumulated depreciation)	(2,200)	
Intangible assets		
Total fixed assets	14,348	-
Other Assets		
Deferred income tax		
Other		
Total Other Assets	-	-
Total Assets	**26,222**	**-**

Liabilities and Owner's Equity		
Current Liabilities		
Accounts payable	8,060	
Short-term loans		
Income taxes payable	3,145	
Accrued salaries and wages		
Unearned revenue		
Current portion of long-term debt		
Total current liabilities	11,205	-
Long-Term Liabilities		
Long-term debt	3,450	
Deferred income tax		
Other		
Total long-term liabilities	3,450	-
Owner's Equity		
Owner's investment	7,178	
Retained earnings	4,389	
Other		
Total owner's equity	11,567	-
Total Liabilities and Owner's Equity	**26,222**	**-**

Common Financial Ratios		
Debt Ratio (Total Liabilities / Total Assets)	0.56	
Current Ratio (Current Assets / Current Liabilities)	1.06	
Working Capital (Current Assets - Current Liabilities)	669	-
Assets-to-Equity Ratio (Total Assets / Owner's Equity)	2.27	
Debt-to-Equity Ratio (Total Liabilities / Owner's Equity)	1.27	

Income Statements

The second part of a GAAP-compliant financial statement is the income statement. People often use the term "bottom line" in reference to the final cost of something or the final result of some type of analysis. This term is actually taken from the income statement, because the final assessment of how much money a company made for a given period of time will always be located on the bottom line of the income statement. Unlike balance sheets, income statements report financial activity over a period of time – usually either an entire financial year, or a financial quarter. The income statement shows all the profit and all the expenses the company earned for that period; sometimes, it may be referred to as a profit and loss statement.

The income statement includes very specific information about a company's income and expenses. For example, income is divided into operating income, non-operating income, and other income. Operating income is all the money a company earned as a result of performing its main business functions. For example, if you own a restaurant, operating income is all the money you earn from preparing and selling meals. Non-operating income is money earned through means that are not the direct result of the business's main focus. For example, the following types of income may be considered non-operating income:

- Interest earned from money deposited in bank accounts;
- Rental income from properties the business may own.

Other income is income earned from financial activity completely unrelated to the business's main function. Examples of other income include:

- Money earned from the sale of real estate, vehicles, or other fixed assets.
- Money earned from the sale of subsidiaries.

The income statement also specifies all the different types of operating expenses the company incurred. Expenses are separated into two categories, as well – primary expenses and secondary expenses. Primary expenses are all the expenses directly related to the production of goods and services sold and to the general administrative costs of running the business. Primary expenses may include:

- Cost of Goods Sold (COGS)
- Research and development
- Employee wages
- Utility and transportation bills
- Depreciation (the loss of value of machinery and equipment used to produce goods and services)

Secondary expenses are indirectly related to the main business operations and may include costs such as:

- Interest paid on loans
- Debts
- Losses associated with the sale of assets

Finally, like all GAAP-compliant financial statements, income statements must follow a predetermined format to report a company's quarterly or annual income. You can think of the income statement as a reverse pyramid, with the big, wide base at the top. At the tops of the statement, you will see the company's "gross income" or gross revenue." This is just the big, unrefined number that results from adding up all the sources of income over the quarter or year.

The next part of the statement shows the expense resulting from income the company may not collect due to sales, discounts, or other reasons. This deduction may be called the "cost of sales" and deducting it from the gross income results in the "net income" or "net revenue."

Operating expenses are detailed next. All the operating expenses are listed, with specific costs associated with each type of expense. Generally, this is where the company will list all the administrative costs of its business operations. By deducting operating expenses from gross profit, you result in a figure called, "income from operations."

Non-operating income and expenses are generally detailed next. These are usually either income or expenses resulting from interest earned or paid; investment returns; or dividends paid out. Some income statements separate interest income and expenses; other statements may combine them. The final amount of this calculation is combined with the income from operations and results in operating profit before tax.

The final step in the income statement process is deducting income tax. The amount of income tax the company paid for the quarter or year is entered here. It is deducted from the operating profit before tax, and the result is net income, net profit, or net earnings. It will be located on the bottom line of the income statement.

The following is an example of an income statement:

[Company Name]   **Income Statement**
For the Years Ending [Dec 31, 2016 and Dec 31, 2017]

Revenue	2017	2016
Sales revenue	110,000	95,000
(Less sales returns and allowances)		
Service revenue	70,000	62,000
Interest revenue		
Other revenue		
Total Revenues	**180,000**	**157,000**

Expenses		
Advertising	1,000	1,000
Bad debt		
Commissions		
Cost of goods sold	65,000	63,000
Depreciation		
Employee benefits		
Furniture and equipment		8,000
Insurance		
Interest expense	4,200	5,200
Maintenance and repairs		
Office supplies		
Payroll taxes		
Rent		
Research and development		
Salaries and wages	55,000	55,000
Software		
Travel		
Utilities		
Web hosting and domains		
Other	17,460	
Total Expenses	**142,660**	**132,200**
Net Income Before Taxes	37,340	24,800
Income tax expense	14,936	9,920
Income from Continuing Operations	**22,404**	**14,880**

Below-the-Line Items		
Income from discontinued operations		
Effect of accounting changes		
Extraordinary items		
Net Income	**22,404**	**14,880**

Cash Flow Statements

Finally, the cash flow statement (CFS) completes the three major parts of a financial statement. As we have seen, the balance sheet provides a snapshot of a company's current assets and liabilities. The income statement provides documentation of a company's profitability. The cash flow statements complete this picture of financial activity by showing not only what a company is worth or whether it has been profitable in the previous financial period, but whether it has been able to generate cash to support its business operations. Like the income statement, the CFS shows changes over a period of time, but the CFS focuses on the net increase or decrease in available cash for a company's business operations. The CFS is divided into three sections: operating activities; investing activities; and financing activities. The net increase or decrease in available cash is shown in the bottom line of the CFS.

- ## Operating Activities

The operating activities section of the CFS documents all activity related to sources or uses of cash resulting from the main operating concern of the business. So, cash from operating activities may include changes to cash accounts, accounts receivable, inventory, accounts payable, wages, income tax, and other operating expenses like rent, depreciation, and interest payments. Essentially, the Operating Activities section of the CFS reconciles the net income for the Income Statement to the amount of actual cash the company has received from its business operations.

- ## Investing Activities

This section of the CFS documents all cash flow related to investment activity. For example, if a company purchases long-term fixed assets, such as land, buildings, plants, and equipment, the Investing Activities section of the CFS shows the outflow of cash used to make the investments. Similarly, if a company sells any of its assets or securities investments, the proceeds would be recorded in this section of the CFS.

• Financing Activities

This section of the CFS records all changes in cash flow resulting from activity related to financing. For example, cash raised as a result of selling shares to stockholders or borrowing money from banks appears in this section of the CFS. In addition, any changes in cash flow resulting from loan payments or other money owed for financed investments would also show up here.

The following is an example of a Cash Flow Statement:

[Company Name]
Cash Flow Statement

For the Year Ending	12/31/15
Cash at Beginning of Year	15,700

Operations

Cash receipts from	
Customers	693,200
Other Operations	
Cash paid for	
Inventory purchases	(264,000)
General operating and administrative expenses	(112,000)
Wage expenses	(123,000)
Interest	(13,500)
Income taxes	(32,800)
Net Cash Flow from Operations	147,900

Investing Activities

Cash receipts from	
Sale of property and equipment	33,600
Collection of principal on loans	
Sale of investment securities	
Cash paid for	
Purchase of property and equipment	(75,000)
Making loans to other entities	
Purchase of investment securities	
Net Cash Flow from Investing Activities	(41,400)

Financing Activities

Cash receipts from	
Issuance of stock	
Borrowing	
Cash paid for	
Repurchase of stock (treasury stock)	
Repayment of loans	(34,000)
Dividends	(53,000)
Net Cash Flow from Financing Activities	(87,000)

Net Increase in Cash	19,500

Cash at End of Year	35,200

Chapter 5: Ledger for

Bookkeeping

The first four chapters of this book have outlined many of the basic principles of bookkeeping. In addition, Chapter 4 discusses financial statements, which provide a standardized and accepted method of presenting the information recorded by a bookkeeper to potential investors, shareholders, and financial regulators. Understanding these basic principles is essential to ensuring that your company's financial records are accurate and reliable. However, the initial chapters of this book have focused more on the end-result of bookkeeping rather than the day-to-day practice of recording transactions throughout a given fiscal period, so that when the end of the quarter or year arrives, your books will be balanced and ready for closing, and all the necessary information will be available for your accountant to prepare financial statements.

The remainder of this book focuses on the details of keeping and maintaining accurate financial records as part of your effort to run an efficient and profitable business venture. This chapter focuses on the two most important depositories of bookkeeping records: the financial journal and the general ledger. Traditionally, both the journal and the ledger were always bound, paper volumes with pages designed specifically to enable the accurate recording of transactions. Because these volumes were always in book form, the term "bookkeeping" was used to describe the profession of maintaining financial records.

As a result of digital technology, many companies now use computer software to record transactions. Although these software applications offer many advantages, such as the ability to search for transactions or simpler entry of information about transactions, the digital versions of these volumes of bookkeeping data have retained the same names – journals and ledgers. In fact, in most cases, even large corporations who depend on the efficiency of automated bookkeeping software have found that to some degree, recording transactions by hand in paper volumes will always be a necessary element of bookkeeping.

Perhaps more importantly, understanding the underlying foundation of how paper journals and ledgers function and their main purpose in keeping accurate transaction records will give you a better understanding of professional bookkeeping. Digital technology has provided the means to automate many of these functions; however, the basic practice of professional bookkeeping remains the same. Attempting to take shortcuts by using financial management software without first understanding GAAP-complaint bookkeeping practices can lead to potentially serious complications.

What is a Ledger?

	A	B	C	D	E	F	G	H	I	J	K
1	General ledger example										
2											
3	General ledger example codes										
4	Budget Line Codes				Project Codes						
5	Grants Disbursment	0			Organizational Management	1					
6	Staff	10			Editing Workshop	2					
7	Food	20			Education Programs	3					
8	Equipment	30			GLAM	4					
9	Travel	40			Communications	5					
10	External Contract	50									
11	Contract Labor	51									
12	Contract Services	52									
13											
14	What you see in the general ledger										
15	Date	Account	Payee or Payor		Memo			Amount	Budget	Project	
16	11/5/2014	Checking	Wikimedia Foundation		Grant for November workshop			$150.00	0	2	
17	11/10/2014	Checking	Smith Library		Snacks for November 2014 workshop			-$25.00	20	2	
18	11/10/2014	Checking	Smith Library		Projector rental for November 2014 workshop			-$10.00	30	2	
19	11/11/2014	Checking	Beatrice Rodriguez		Bookkeeping contractor			-$109.41	52	1	
20	11/12/2014	Checking	Chen Repair Services		Fix damaged screen			-$62.25	30	1	
21	11/14/2014	Checking	Igor Flintrov		Salary for November 2014 workshop			-$113.18	51	1	
22	11/14/2014	Checking	Igor Flintrov		Salary for education programs support			-$540.73	51	3	
23	11/17/2014	Checking	Wikimedia Foundation		Return excess grant funds			-$1.82	0	2	
24											
25	Calculating the total costs for November 2014 workshop										
26			Salary	$113.18							
27			Snacks	$25.00							
28			Projector rental	$10.00							
29			Total	$148.18	The formula for this "Total" cell is =SUM(D26,D28)						
30											
31	Cost-effectiveness measures for the November 2014 workshop										
32					Number	Cost per each					
33		New editors			15	-$9.88	The formula for this "Cost per each" cell is =IFERROR($D$29/E33, "Not applicable")				
34		New articles			4	-$37.05	The formula for this "Cost per each" cell is =IFERROR($D$29/E34, "Not applicable")				
35		Files created			36	-$4.12	The formula for this "Cost per each" cell is =IFERROR($D$29/E35, "Not applicable")				
36		Edits made			207	-$0.72	The formula for this "Cost per each" cell is =IFERROR($D$29/E36, "Not applicable")				
37		Quality images included in new files			2	-$74.09	The formula for this "Cost per each" cell is =IFERROR($D$29/E37, "Not applicable")				
38		Valued images included in new files			0	Not applicable	The formula for this "Cost per each" cell is =IFERROR($D$29/E38, "Not applicable")				
39		Featured pictures included in new files			0	Not applicable	The formula for this "Cost per each" cell is =IFERROR($D$29/E39, "Not applicable")				

Figure 6: Free Image

In bookkeeping, a ledger is a book or record of financial accounts, with transaction data taken from the journal, then re-organized with all transaction entries sorted by account type rather than transaction date. Also called a general ledger, this record of accounts is organized according to the five main types of accounts – asset accounts; liability accounts; equity accounts; revenue accounts; and expense accounts.

The ledger is the centerpiece of the entire accounting cycle. Chapter 3 discussed how the chart of accounts (COA) lists all of the accounts, by type, that a company uses to keep track of its financial records. The general ledger represents all activity in every account listed in the COA. Every account listed in the COA will always have a balance, and that balance can be found by looking at the transaction records listed in the general ledger. So, if an employee wants to know the current available balance in petty cash, the general ledger will provide that information.

All the accounts listed in the COA are presented in the ledger in a standardized format the accommodates double-entry bookkeeping. Standard paper ledgers all use a T-Account entry that allows the bookkeeper to enter a debt and a credit for every transaction.

The following examples show how T-accounts are used to record transaction in a general ledger. In the first example, an expense account (rent) and a liability account (accounts payable) are debited and credited; in the second example, liability account (accounts payable) and an asset account (cash) are debited and credited. Even if your general ledger is kept in a computer database, the visual interface you use to enter account transaction information is likely to appear as a T-account.

Rent Expense					Accounts Payable			
Debit		Credit			Debit		Credit	
Date	Amt	Date	Amt		Date	Amt	Date	Amt
7/01	$10,000.00						7/01	$10,000.00
Bal $10,000.00							Bal $10,000.00	

Accounts Payable					Cash			
Debit		Credit			Debit		Credit	
Date	Amt	Date	Amt		Date	Amt	Date	Amt
7/06	$10,000.00						7/06	$10,000.00
Bal $10,000.00							Bal $10,000.00	

Here is another example of how T-accounts in a general ledger are used to allow a bookkeeper to record changes to the balance of an asset account, in this case a company's cash account:

Acct 101	CASH ON HAND		Balance
	Debits	Credits	(DR Bal)
1-Sep-14			$6,040
5-Sep-14	$4,200	$1,180	$9,060
6-Sep-14	$5,800		$14,860
6-Sep-14	$1,200		$16,060

Why Use a Ledger?

The general ledger provides comprehensive transaction information, including transaction history and its effect on the current balance for that category of account. As a result, because the general ledger places transactions into the proper accounting context, the ledger is used as the most authoritative source of financial information for a company. In a GAAP-compliant accounting system, there are generally five steps in the accounting cycle:

1. Business transactions occur.
2. Transactions are recorded as entries in journals.
3. Journal entries are transferred to ledgers.
4. Trial balances are created using the information in ledgers.
5. Ledgers are used to create financial statements.

Although ledgers do not enter the accounting cycle until the third step, they serve several extremely important functions:

- They allow bookkeepers and accountants to ensure the balances of every account in the COA are accurately adjusted to reflect the most recent transactions.

- They allow the accounting team, by creating trail balances, to ensure that all debts and credits for each account are equal. This step allows the accounting team to locate and correct bookkeeping errors prior to ending the fiscal year.

- They provide the source of the information that is presented in annual financial statements.

Modern corporations that employ large numbers of people in many locations, all of whom communicate using digital communication tools, may engage in transactions and record journal entries around-the-clock. This king of high-volume business activity presents even greater opportunities for bookkeeping errors, lost revenue and profitability, and potentially catastrophic accounting and tax liability concerns. By using a general ledger to maintain accurate account balances, those same digital tools can be used to ensure accountability and accuracy and increase the overall efficiency and effectiveness of the bookkeeping system.

The Nitty-Gritty About Journals and Ledgers

The previous sections' discussion general ledgers included references to financial journals. Financial journals are related to ledgers, but they are separate records that serve an entirely different purpose. As mentioned earlier in this book, the purpose of bookkeeping is to record every transaction in which a business engages. Financial statements provide the final accounting of these records for any given period of time, and these records are derived directly from the information maintained in the general ledger.

However, business transactions rarely follow such a neat and organized pattern, so bookkeepers must have a way of keeping track of transactions as they occur. This is the second step of the accounting cycle, and financial journals are used to maintain these records.

Like general ledgers, general journals traditionally take the form of paper-based notebooks or bound volumes. They contain page after page of transaction entries, all listed in chronological order. Because the journal is the place where transactions are first recorded, they are sometimes called the book of original entry. A journal entry will include detailed information about the transaction, such as the date, the accounts that should be debited and credited, and a description of the purpose of the transaction. Depending on the size and complexity of the company, the bookkeeping department may require the use of several types of journals, each designated for specific purposes – for example, purchase transaction journals, cash receipt journals, sales transaction journals, etc. Companies who use specialized journals may also utilize a general journal to record less frequently occurring transactions, like depreciation or interest.

One of the primary differences between journals and ledgers is that the information is journals is entered chronologically and by individual transaction. This information would require a lot of additional analysis to produce financial statements or to ensure that the accounts are all balanced; however, this format data entry allows bookkeepers and accountants to locate individual transactions more easily, and this feature can be very important to the overall effort to maintain accurate, balanced accounts.

For example, consider that the general ledgers provide the most authoritative view of all account information – the ledger shows the relationship of account balances to transactions. Before creating financial statements, the general ledger is used to create trial balances that can allow an accountant to determine whether the accounts are balanced – i.e., that credit and debits are equal across all accounts and account types. The importance of journals becomes apparent when accounts are out of balance. Although the ledger may indicate where the imbalance occurs, the journal holds the information about each individual transaction. This information can allow financial regulators and accountants to locate the source of the inaccuracy, correct the imbalance, and close the books at the end of the fiscal period.

The following is an example of how chronological entries may appear in a financial journal:

Date	Account Name	Debit	Credit
Feb 1, 2018	Cash	100,750	
	Bonds Payable		100,000
	Interest Payable		750
Feb 28, 2018	Interest Expense	750	
	Interest Payable		750
Mar 31, 2018	Interest Expense	750	
	Interest Payable		750
Apr 30, 2018	Interest Expense	750	
	Interest Payable		750
May 31, 2018	Interest Expense	750	
	Interest Payable		750
Jun 30, 2018	Interest Expense	750	
	Interest Payable		750
Jun 30, 2018	Interest Payable	4,500	
	Cash		4,500
Jul 31, 2018	Interest Expense	750	
	Interest Payable		750
Aug 31, 2018	Interest Expense	750	
	Interest Payable		750
Sep 30, 2018	Interest Expense	750	
	Interest Payable		750
Oct 31, 2018	Interest Expense	750	
	Interest Payable		750
Nov 30, 2018	Interest Expense	750	
	Interest Payable		750
Dec 31, 2018	Interest Expense	750	
	Interest Payable		750
Dec 31, 2018	Interest Payable	4,500	
	Cash		4,500

How to Input Data into a Ledger

Generally, transaction records should not be entered directly into an account ledger. The journal is the book of original entry, and this where all transaction records should begin. This distinction is easier to maintain for companies who use paper records. Traditional bookkeeping methods require the use of physically different books, and each book will have pages that are designed for different types of account entries. For example, the following is an example of a blank page from a financial journal. Notice how the page is specifically designed to accept chronological entries of transactions, with a description and an indication of whether it should be entered into the ledger as a debit or credit:

GENERAL JOURNAL

DATE	ACCOUNT NAME	DEBIT	CREDIT

By contrast, the following sample of a T-account page from a ledger looks completely different. The ledger page is designed to accept only entries affecting accounts receivable. The date of the transaction, space to indicate the type of transaction, and the amount the account should be debited or credited. The specific information entered into the T-account page is taken from the journal, where it was originally recorded.

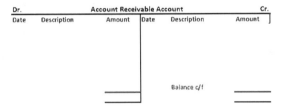

Of course, even companies that still maintain paper-based records usually use some type of bookkeeping software to help make entries more accurate, consistent, and traceable. For the most part, advances in bookkeeping technology have made the job of maintaining accurate records easier, more efficient, and less prone to error. However, automation has also resulted in some fundamental changes to the way bookkeeping entries may be made.

The primary difference between paper-based bookkeeping and automated bookkeeping is that paper-based records require physically different books to record transactions, while computer software may incorporate both journals and ledgers into the same program. This arrangement simplifies the concepts of journals and ledgers; in fact, many software applications do not even use the concepts of journals and ledgers, opting instead for a variety of user-interface windows that allow for various types of data entry functions. Although the software may make a distinction about the database in which certain data is stored based on the form or window used to enter the information, bookkeeping personnel who have been trained exclusively in these environments may believe that all transaction records are entered directly into the ledger. Although this confusion may not affect the ability of the bookkeeper to enter accurate data, understanding that journals and ledgers provide two different methods of recording business transactions is important when it is time to balance the books and produce accurate financial statements. The following are some of the fundamental difference between journal and ledgers:

Journals vs. Ledgers		
	Journal	Ledger
Definition	Journals are used as the first point of recording a financial transaction.	Ledgers use a T-format to record credits and balances by account type and supply date for financial statements.
Importance	The accuracy of journals is more important. The accuracy of the ledger depends on the accuracy of the journal.	The ledger depends on the transactions in the journal to produce financial statements.
Format	Simple format, date, descriptions, and transaction	More complex accounting input, with account type

	amount.	and debits and credits for both sides
Alternate title	The book of original entry.	The book of second entry.
Entry terminology	Entering transactions in a journal is called journalizing.	Entering transactions in a ledger is called posting.
Method of record-keeping	Chronological	According to account
Balancing	Journals do not need to be balanced.	Ledgers must be balanced.

Different Types of Ledgers

As discussed throughout this section journals and ledgers each serve important roles in maintaining accurate and reliable records of any business's transaction details. The general principles of bookkeeping apply across the board regardless of what type of journal or ledger you use, or whether you are utilizing a digital software or a paper-based system. However, there are still many differences among the many types of ledgers and journals companies may use.

There are three types of ledgers used in professional bookkeeping:

- General ledger
- Debtors ledger
- Creditors ledger

General Ledger

The general ledger (GL), as discussed above, contains all the transactions of the business, organized according to the five standard account types – assets, liabilities, equities, revenue, and expenses. Some companies that use a general ledger may also incorporate into the main ledger additional sub-ledgers, such as a nominal ledger or a private ledger. The nominal ledger contains transaction information for accounts that are less directly involved in the main function of the business – for example, salaries, rent, office supplies, insurance, and depreciation. The private ledger contains transaction information that is confidential, such as information about salaries and capital investments.

Debtors' Ledger

The debtors' ledger is also known as a sales ledger. These types of ledgers are used to record all transactions relating to customers who have purchased goods or services on credit. Companies who have the capacity to extend credit will maintain a debtors' ledger. This ledger will contain information about the total sum of money owed to the business. Accounts will be organized into categories such as Accounts Receivable, Trade Debtors, and Sundry Debtors. Traditionally, accounts in these types of ledger are organized alphabetically, although modern software has enabled a variety of search and sort functions.

Creditors' Ledger

The creditors' ledger records all transaction information related to sellers from whom goods or services have been purchased on credit. This ledger will contain information such as the total sum of money owed by a business to all individuals and organizations from whom they have made purchases that have not yet been paid. Account types in a creditors' ledger may include Accounts Payable, Trade Creditors, and Sundry Creditors. The values for each account of the creditors' ledger will appear in the appropriate area of the balance sheet when the accountant creates the trial balance.

Chapter 6: Essential Guide to

Bookkeeping

The first five chapters of this book have covered many of the basic concepts of standardized, GAAP-compliant bookkeeping. By now, you should be feeling much more comfortable thinking about the basic skills and concerns you will have to address to ensure your company's bookkeeping is accurate, reliable, consistent, and up to professional standards. If you are assembling a bookkeeping system for yourself or for a client company, having a solid foundation in bookkeeping fundamentals is important.

This chapter pulls all that information together to give you an overview of everything you should consider before making any decisions about hiring a bookkeeper, building a system, or outsourcing your bookkeeping needs. The information in this chapter is divided into three sections:

- Startup Considerations
- Procedures During the Fiscal Period
- Procedures for the End of the Fiscal Period

Figure 7: Free Image

Startup Considerations

The bookkeeping and accounting system that any company uses should represent a long-term commitment resulting from a methodical and thorough examination of the company's current size and complexity, as well as its prospects and plans for future growth and development. One of the most important aspects in which accurate and reliable bookkeeping shows its value is tax filing. Depending on the size and complexity of your business concerns, the Internal Revenue Service (IRS) may require that you indicate which type of accounting and bookkeeping system your company uses; making changes to these agreements can be time-consuming, costly, and difficult, so it pays to think things through ahead of time. In addition, you; your investors and shareholders; your customer base; potential future investors; lenders; and financial regulators may request an examination or even an audit of your books. Producing reliable financial statements requires a disciplined and consistent method of bookkeeping so that changes in profit, loss, and equity over time can be more effectively and easily tracked. Thus, by choosing a bookkeeping and accounting system that is most appropriate for your business venture, you will be taking the right steps toward ensuring successful and profitable business administration.

Choosing a Bookkeeping System

As discussed earlier in this book, there are two recognized systems of GAAP-compliant bookkeeping: single-entry and double-entry. We will explore the pros and cons of both systems in this section. We will also discuss the strengths and weaknesses of online, web-based, and digital bookkeeping systems.

Single-entry Bookkeeping

A single-entry bookkeeping system is the most informal of all bookkeeping systems. If you have a checking account, the check register is a great example of single-entry bookkeeping. All the transactions in the check registry provide information about only the one checking account. Whether the transaction is a deposit resulting for a business transaction; from a personal or professional investment; from a business or personal loan; or from interest paid on the account or dividends received from investments in securities, all the transactions are listed chronologically, with a small space for description of the transaction, and a column on the right to show how the transaction affected the balance in the account.

Withdrawals are tracked the same way – whether a withdrawal results from a direct withdrawal from the bank for personal or business use; for payment of a bill for operating expenses for your business; form a purchase made for equipment or office supplies; from payments for loans, interest, or taxes; or from the purchase of investments, all the transactions will be listed chronologically; again with a small space for a description of the transaction; and a column on the right to show how the transaction affected the balance.

This method of bookkeeping is fairly straightforward and can be an effective means of showing accurately where money comes in and goes out each month. However, with the prevalence of online banking, we have all encountered the difficulty of keeping track of all transactions in a simple check register. Previous top widespread access to online banking, most deposit transactions were made in person at the bank, and most withdrawals were conducted by mailed checks. This level of control over financial activity made the single-entry system a more viable option for individuals and businesses over a much broader range of business contexts. The contemporary environment requires a reassessment of whether a single-entry system is right for you.

Advantages:

- Single-entry bookkeeping uses a simple and easy-to-understand method of keeping track of transactions.

- Small businesses that have only one major financial account may be able to save time and expense by using this system effectively.
- A single-entry system can be adapted for larger companies by creating separate single-entry systems for each business account.

Disadvantages:

- Single-entry systems do not provide a means of including detailed financial reporting.
- Bookkeeping errors can be very difficult to locate and usually involve reconciling bookkeeping records with bank statements.
- Single-entry systems do not provide an effective means of creating projections of future financial performance.
- Single-entry systems generally track only cash accounts. Other assets, as well as liabilities, equity, income, and expenses go unreported in these systems.

Double-entry Bookkeeping

Especially in a globalized, digital environment, it is common even for small, local businesses to have many accounts with different suppliers, service providers, and customers, often from different locations and even different countries. In addition, the increasingly self-service nature of investing and business administration can mean that even small businesses may have to take on considerably greater responsibility than in previous eras. Regardless, the larger and more complex your business, the more likely a double-entry system will allow you to consistently maintain reliable books. Most companies use the double-entry system.

In the section above, we used the analogy of a check register to describe the single-entry system. Using a double-entry system, the transactions in the previous example represent only half of the entire bookkeeping process. For example, if you made a deposit into your checking account for payments received from customers for good and services sold, the record of the deposit into the checking account (a single-entry) is only half of the transaction record; in order to balance the books, there needs to be a second-entry is a corresponding account. The idea behind double-entry systems is that putting money into one account necessarily means that money was taken from another account and vice-versa. Double-entry bookkeeping allows you to show both sides of the transaction. So, when a company makes a deposit resulting from sales, revenue can be credited for the same amount the checking account was debited, which results in a balanced record of the transaction. Similarly, if the business owner pays an outstanding bill for shipping, the double-entry system will record a credit to the checking account and a debit to the accounts payable.

Advantages:

- Provides a more complete system of recording all of a company's financial transactions, not just deposits and withdrawals to the main checking account.

- Provides a means of producing accurate and reliable financial statements.

- Provides an effective means of pinpointing internal accounting errors.
- Provides a means of accurately assessing a company's financial condition.

Disadvantages:
- Double-entry bookkeeping is more complex and may take more time to learn.

Choosing an Accounting Method

As there are two officially recognized methods of bookkeeping, so there are two officially recognized methods of accounting:

- Cash accounting
- Accrual accounting

Also similar to bookkeeping methods, choosing the most appropriate type of accounting method for your business will involve an assessment of the size and complexity of your business. This section examines the two different types of accounting methods, including advantages and disadvantages.

Cash Accounting

Cash accounting is fairly straightforward. It is called cash accounting because transactions are only recorded at the time cash changes hands. For example, in a business that uses cash-based accounting, a sale is recorded in the books at the time payment is received from the customer. Similarly, expenses are only recorded at the time the business actually makes a payment for a purchase or to pay a bill.

Advantages and Disadvantages:

Small businesses, such as sole proprietorships and limited partnerships, often use a cash accounting system, particularly when they do not have any inventory. The clear advantage to the cash accounting system is that it provides a very simple and straightforward method of recognizing when revenue has been received and when expenses have been paid. In addition, when using a cash accounting system, businesses do not pay taxes on income until is received.

However, a disadvantage is that using a cash accounting system does not allow a business to match its revenue and expenses in time. For example, if a construction business wins a contract in January and completes it in June, revenue is recorded in June when payment is received, even though the contract was signed in January. Similarly, if the same business receives an insurance bill due in quarterly installment, the expense is only recorded when the payments are made, rather than as an annual expense. the in its rent of $1,000 per month for the entire year in January, it would have to record a $12,000 expense in January, rather than distributing the payments throughout the year.

Accrual Accounting

Accrual accounting is more complex. It is called accrual accounting because transactions are recorded at the time they are earned or incurred, rather than when they are paid for. For example, consider a construction business that uses accrual accounting. The business may make a sale in January, but the contract may not be completed until June. Using accrual accounting, the business can record the sale in January, rather than waiting until June. Similarly, a company using accrual accounting records all the money it owes as current transactions in accounts payable, rather than waiting to record each bill as it is paid.

if the same business prepays rent on its facilities for the entire year in January, each of the monthly rent payments can be recorded as paid for the entire upcoming year, even though each of the rental installments may not yet have been deposited by the property manager.

Advantages and Disadvantages:

The accrual method is generally used by larger business. In fact, if a business generates over $5 million in annual revenue, the IRS requires that they use accrual accounting. The clear advantage to the accrual accounting system is that it provides a more accurate picture of the company's financial condition by allowing a business to match its revenue and expenses in time. For example, if a construction business wins a contract in January and completes it in June, revenue in an accrual system is recorded in January when the contract is signed, rather than waiting for payment in June, when the work is completed. Similarly, a company using accrual accounting can record at the beginning of the year the total amount of an annual insurance bill due in quarterly installment, rather than waiting to submit payments once a quarter.

To illustrate how this difference can affect the assessment of a company's financial picture, imagine that the construction company who won the contract in January wanted to apply for a business loan. Using cash accounting, a lender may be less willing to invest in the business because they cannot show earnings for the recently signed contract.

Similarly, a business using cash accounting that prepays its rent of $1,000 per month for the entire year in January would have to record a $12,000 expense in January, with no rent payments for the rest of the year; accrual accounting would allow the same business to distribute the expense throughout the year. Although the total rent expense for the year is the same, anyone examining the cash flow statement for either company at any given time may get a skewed picture of the company's overall performance.

Changing Accounting Methods

Cash accounting allows businesses to defer taxes by delaying the deposit of revenue. This may appeal to many businesses, particularly when they have large earnings at the end of the year. However, to avoid artificially inflated or deflated financial statements that can affect the health of the market, the IRS requires all businesses to state which type of accounting method they use. You also have to notify the IRS if you decide to change your accounting method by filing a Form 3115.

Here is a summary of the differences between the cash and accrual accounting:

Cash Accounting	Accrual Accounting
Recognizes revenue at the time it is received.	Recognizes revenue at the time it is earned (i.e., when an invoice or contract is completed),
Recognizes expenses at the time they are paid.	Recognizes expenses at the time they are billed (i.e., when the company receives an invoice).

Taxes are deferred on revenue that has not yet been received.	Taxes must be paid on revenue and accounts receivable.
Mostly used by small businesses and sole proprietors with no inventory.	Required for businesses with revenue over $5 million.

Procedures During the Fiscal Period

Now that you have decided on a bookkeeping system and an accounting method, the real work of recording your company's transactions can begin. There are a ton of resources available wherever you look – television, radio, print, and online service companies and independent operators all know there is money to be made in the gig economy simply by providing helpful advice and guidance in the day-to-day operation of a small business. A lot of these sources provide valuable information, but not all of it is dependable. This section will provide a general overview of some of the most important concerns you should be addressing as you establish an effective and reliable bookkeeping system.

Tracking Income and Expenses

Before you even think about producing or analyzing financial statements or tax documents, you need to establish a system of recording your day-to-day expenses. The law does not specify exactly how you should go about the process of recording your daily transactions and receipts or compiling your monthly or annual financial records. However, there are established bookkeeping and accounting methods that you must use. The best way to begin formulating a bookkeeping system that works for you is to simply visit your local office supply store and buy a journal and a ledger to record your daily transactions. A single-entry cash accounting system can be an effective method of tracking expenses for a small startup company; if your company grows, you can adapt the bookkeeping and accounting methods to address those changes. If you have a business checking account, you may also use a business checkbook to record transactions.

The following is a list of all the types of books that may be required for a recordkeeping system for a small business:

- business checkbook
- journals to record the following:
  - daily summary of cash receipts
  - check disbursements journal
  - monthly summary of cash receipts

- ○   depreciation worksheet
- ○   employee compensation record
- a general ledger to record how the transactions in the journals are reflected in the business checking account.

Alternatively, you may use computer software to track your expenses and receipts. These software programs are usually fairly easy to use and may require little knowledge of bookkeeping to begin making entries. Chapter 10 examines QuickBooks and other online and digital bookkeeping applications.

Organizing Documents

Once you have decided how you will be recording your business's daily, weekly, and monthly transactions, you must have some idea of what types of expenses you will be tracking. The importance of keeping receipts, invoices, paid bills, deposit slips, canceled checks, and bank statements is that they provide support for the numbers you enter into your bookkeeping and accounting system. The accuracy of this information is important because it affects the accuracy of the information in your tax returns and can help you resolve inquiries from auditors, the IRS, as well as support claims of creditworthiness on loan applications.

The following are the types of transaction records you should be recording, separated into 4 main categories:

- Gross receipts. All receipts of business income resulting from sales of goods or services fall under the category of gross receipts. Transaction records should show dates, amounts received and sources. Examples of gross receipts include:
  - cash register tapes
  - bank deposit slips
  - receipt book slips
  - invoices
  - credit card charge slips and receipts
  - IRS forms 1099-MISC
- Inventory. Inventory refers to all items purchased and resold to customers, including raw materials used to produce finished items. Records of inventory transactions should show the amount paid and an indication that it was purchased for inventory. Inventory records may include:
  - cancelled checks
  - cash register receipts
  - credit/debit card sales receipts
  - invoices from suppliers

- Expenses. Records of all costs incurred to run your business (except for inventory) should go here. These records should show the amount and date paid with some indication that it was a business-related expense. Transaction records may include:

  - cancelled checks
  - cash register receipts
  - credit/debit card sales receipts
  - account statements for service suppliers
  - invoices
  - petty cash receipts for per diem expenses

- Assets. As discussed earlier, assets include all property owned by the business that has some type of practical value for the business. Asset records should not only show purchase price but also track depreciation and losses or gains when the assets are sold. Any of the following documents may show this information:

  - purchase and sales invoices
  - real estate closing statements
  - canceled checks or other transaction receipts

Organizing Deductions

When you file income tax at the end of the year, you should be able to deduct the expenses associated with running your business from the total revenue earned. When you report a lower total revenue, you will be less in taxes. The following are the types of business expenses the IRS allows you to deduct on our tax returns:

- Business start-up costs. The types of costs associated with start-ups vary depending on the type of business but may include:

  - advertising
  - travel
  - surveys
  - training
  - asset purchases

- Depreciation. If you purchased assets that will last longer than one year, you can claim as start-up expenses. However, you can claim the value of depreciation for such assets. Typically, asset depreciation is claimed for the following types of assets:

  - office furniture
  - buildings
  - equipment and machinery

- Business use of home. If your home is your principal place of business, you may be able to claim certain tax deductions, but you will have to provide documentation that shows:

  - what business services are performed at your home.
  - how your home has been converted to business use.

- Car and truck expenses. Keeping accurate records of your car and truck usage can also help you find ways to save money. The following types of business-related travel expenses are deductible:

  - depreciation
  - lease payments
  - registration
  - garage rent
  - licenses
  - repairs
  - gas
  - oil
  - tires
  - insurance
  - parking fees
  - tolls

Invoicing Customers

One of the primary transaction records you will be maintaining is sales revenue, under gross receipts. As a result, ensuring that your business has a reliable system of invoicing is essential.

- ## Standard invoices

For your general bookkeeping needs, you can purchase not only journals and ledgers at your local office supply store but also invoice books. You may also wish to create company invoices that match your company letterhead. Regardless, you should record every invoice you send in one journal, and all paid invoices in another journal, with monthly balances transferred to the ledger as either revenue or accounts receivable.

• Electronic Invoices

Chapter 10 discusses QuickBooks and other digital and web-based bookkeeping and accounting systems. Many – if not all – of these systems offer some type of invoicing function. Many businesses choose this system because the invoicing feature will also automatically record the invoice in accounts receivable and provide a method of tracking sent invoices and entering payments when they are received by customers. Other online money transferring applications like PayPal also offer invoicing functions. PayPal and other web-based payment systems can be adapted for business uses. The invoicing features are fairly flexible and allow for customized invoice design, as well as fairly complex reporting systems that can allow business to keep track of invoices sent and payments received. If you use online invoicing as part of your business's bookkeeping and invoicing system, make sure you incorporate all activity associated with your business into your daily, weekly, and monthly bookkeeping records.

Procedures for the End of the Fiscal Period

Throughout the fiscal year, much of your time and effort will be spent producing the goods and services for you your business. At the end of the year, you will have to file your business income taxes. You will also have the opportunity to balance the books and create reports to assess the performance of your business and make decisions about how you intend to move forward.

During the course of the year, you will have to dedicate some of that time to recording all transactions that affect your business's financial condition. The more disciplined, regular, and well-organized your bookkeeping system, the easier it will be for you to prepare end-of-cycle financial statements and records. This section will examine some of those areas in detail.

Closing the Books

"The books" are the records of your company's financial transactions. Whether you keep paper records, digital records, or a combination of both you will compile a lot of information in journals and ledgers as you keep track of your business's activities throughout the year. At the end of the year (or whichever period signals the end of a financial cycle for you), your bookkeeping and accounting team must "close the books." Closing the books means that all of your financial reporting for that period will be finalized. Once the books are closed, no further adjustments will be made to those records, although you will have to keep copies of those records on file for as many as 7 years after closing.

The purpose of closing the books is to ensure that all income and expenses have been accounted for accurately and that all transactions for the current period have been completed or otherwise accounted for. Closing the books also presents businesses with the opportunity to create financial statements that can provide insight into their company's performance, profitability, and efficiency.

Closing the books is a multi-step process. Each of those steps is highlighted below:

1. Transfer journal entries to the general ledger.

Depending on your method of bookkeeping and accounting, you may transfer journal entries into the ledger at the end of each week, each month, each quarter, or at the end of the year. Generally, for companies that keep paper records, transferring journal entries into the ledger once a month is common practice.

If your company uses bookkeeping software, your journal entries may be automatically transferred into the ledger at the point of entry. Alternatively, your software may have features that allow you to manually tell the program when to transfer journal entries into the ledger, or to automate the data transfer.

2. Compile a Preliminary Trial Balance

A trial balance is a worksheet that can be created manually or using bookkeeping software. The trial balance reflects the totals of all the debits and all the credits in all of the accounts included in the ledger. The purpose of the trial balance is to ensure all account entries in the journals and the ledger up to the end of the reporting period were entered accurately by checking the math to see if the debits and credits have equal balances.

To create a preliminary trial balance:

- Add up all the debit and credit transaction totals in every account in the ledger. To balance a ledger account, total all the debits and credits to each account. The resulting totals will be either a debit or credit balance.

- Next, prepare a trial balance worksheet with three columns – one column lists account names from the ledger; one column lists debit balances; and one column lists credit balances.

- Third, write the name of each account from the ledger and its total credit or debit balance in the worksheet. Following is an example of a trial balance worksheet:

Trial Balance
XYZ Trading
as at 30 June 2010

General Ledger Accounts	[Dr.-Debit]	[Cr.-Credit]
Cash at bank	10,000	
Inventory	40,000	
Vehicles	30,000	
Fixtures & Fittings	32,000	
Accounts Receivable	15,000	
Credit Cards payable		12,000
Accounts Payable		15,000
Bank Loan		50,000
Sales		175,000
Purchases	60,000	
Advertising	5,000	
Wages	65,000	
Rent	15,000	
Electricity	5,000	
Owners Capital		25,000
TOTAL	**277,000**	**277,000**

- Fourth, add the balances in the debit column and write the total at the bottom; then, add the balances in the credit column and write that total at the bottom. If the total debits equal the total credits, your books are balanced.

3.   Add adjusting journal entries.

Accumulation and depreciation should be tracked in a separate journal. These figures should be transferred to the ledger, then added to the trial balance worksheet.

4.   Create an adjusted trial balance.

- After adding the figures for accumulation and depreciation, add the columns of debits and credits again.
- This is the adjusted trial balance. If the total at the bottom of the debit column is the same as the total of the credit column, your books are balanced and ready to close.

5.   Make corrections.

- If the total debit and credit balances are not equal, you will have to locate the bookkeeping errors and make corrections. The following are some areas where errors commonly occur:

- Mistakes transferring amounts from the ledger to the trial balance worksheet.
- Errors in calculating balances of ledger accounts.
- Incorrect amounts posted in the ledger from the journal.
- Debited an account instead of crediting an account, or vice versa.
- Error in entering a transaction in a journal.

- Once you have located the discrepancy and corrected the balance, run the trial balance again until the total debits and credits match.

6. **Generate financial statements.**

- Chapter 4 of this book discusses the three types of financial statements in greater detail:
  - Balance sheet. Remember, the balance sheet shows the company's total assets, liabilities, and equities at the time the report is created.
  - Income statement. The income statement shows how much profit the company generated over the previous accounting cycle by

showing the total revenue left over after all expenses have been deducted.

    ○   Cash flow statement. Finally, the cash flow statement shows how the company generated profit – whether it was generated mostly from selling goods and services or resulted primarily for loans and investments.

- If your company uses bookkeeping software, generating reports and financial statements may be as easy as clicking on a button or selecting a "Create financial statements" option for a dropdown menu. However, the financial statements themselves will only be as valuable as the information in the journals and ledgers from which the software application draws data to create the reports. For this reason, it is important to ensure that you complete all the preliminary steps before attempting to generate final reports.

- Alternatively, you may keep paper-based records. If this is the case, you can use or edit pre-designed templates for each of the three main types of financial statements, then transfer the data from the general ledger directly into the templates. The examples in Chapter 4 illustrate the types of templates that are widely available for this purpose. You can find blank templates using an internet search engine or at your local office supply store.

7. Enter closing entries.

Revenue and expense accounts should be closed with zero balances. Remaining balances should be transferred to permanent accounts such as accounts payable or retained earnings.

8. Generate a final trial balance.

The final trial balance will show the total debits and credits of all the accounts listed on the balance sheet for that accounting period.

Chapter 7: How to Set Up a Single-Entry Bookkeeping System

By now you have read about most of the basic principles involved in basic bookkeeping and accounting for small businesses. To review, the previous chapters have covered the following topics:

- Types of bookkeeping methods:

    o Single-entry
    o Double-entry

- Types of accounting methods:

    o Cash accounting
    o Accrual accounting

- Financial statements:

    o Balance sheets
    o Income statements

- ○ Cash flow statements

- Basic recordkeeping:

  - ○ Financial journals
  - ○ General ledgers
  - ○ Beginning and ending activities for the bookkeeping cycle

Most of these principles are easy enough to understand in theory. However, putting them into practice in your business can be a little more challenging. This chapter and the next will use case studies to illustrate specifically how a business owner can set up and start using a bookkeeping system. This chapter will focus on single-entry bookkeeping that uses cash accounting.

Case Study: Brown Computer Repair

Figure 8: Free Image

Let's assume that Alan and Mary Brown own a computer repair shop. Their business is a sole proprietorship that generates less than $5 million in revenue annually. In addition, because they provide repair services, their business does not maintain an inventory of items for resale. Instead, when a repair job requires additional parts, they order them for that specific contract only. Of course, they do maintain fixed assets that include equipment, office furniture, and other supplies necessary to run their business. The Browns have one part-time employee, Margaret O'Sullivan.

We will use the Browns' computer repair business to illustrate how a single-entry cash accounting system can be used to maintain accurate and reliable records of business transactions. Remember, this example is used for illustration purposes; in actual practice, your business may implement practices much different from this example.

Setting up the Cash Book

The cash book is a journal that records the cash sales, income, and payments made from the cash accounts of the business. The transactions are all recorded in the cash book in chronological order as they occur and balanced on a daily basis. At a regular interval – usually once a month – the results of the transactions recorded in the cash book will be posted to the appropriate cash account in the general ledger.

- ### Daily Summary of Cash Receipts

The Browns' cash book includes a Summary of Cash Receipts to record proceeds for all cash sales for each business day. Throughout the day, the Browns keep track of sales using printouts of online invoices paid, and cash register receipts from in-store sales. At the end of the business day, the Browns add all the money received through sales for that day, including sales tax, and record the amount in the space for total receipts for that day. In this example, the Browns also maintain a Petty Cash fund of $150.00, so they can make small cash purchases without having to access the business checking account. Whenever they make purchases out of the petty cash fund, they issue a receipt, which is included in the total cash receipts for the day. The amount petty cash spent, and the remaining amount in the fund are included in the daily balance. When the fund approaches $0.00, the Browns write check to Petty Cash and restore the find to a $150.00 balance. The check is recorded as a transaction in the Check Payments journal.

On January 7, the Browns totaled all their sales receipts for the day. Altogether, they generated $726.42 in cash sales, plus an additional $61.75 in sales tax. In addition, they had used $42.00 from the petty cash fund to buy cables and adapters. The total of all sales rescripts, plus petty cash receipts, is recorded in the Daily Summary of Cash Receipts in the cashbook, as follows:

Daily Cash Receipts

Daily Summary of Cash Receipts

Date ____ January 7. 20 — _____

Cash sales		726.42
Sales tax		61.75
	TOTAL RECEIPTS	788.17

Cash on hand

Cash in register (including unspent petty cash)

Coins	17.29	
Bills	351 65	
Checks	227.23	
TOTAL CASH IN REGISTER		596.17
Add: Petty cash slips		42.00
	TOTAL CASH	638.17

Less: Change and petty cash

Petty cash slips	42.00	
Coins and bills . . . . (unspent petty cash)	108.00	
TOTAL CHANGE AND PETTY CASH FUND . .		150.00
	TOTAL CASH RECEIPTS	788.17

Monthly Summary of Cash Receipts

Next, the total daily cash receipts recorded in the Daily Summary of Cash Receipts is transferred to the Monthly Summary of Cash Receipts for that day. In the example below, total cash receipts before and after taxes are shown for every business day in January. The column at the far right also shows the record of total deposits made into the business checking account.

Monthly Summary of Cash Receipts

Year 20—   Month January

Day	Net Sales	Sales Tax	Daily Receipts	Deposit
3	413.12	35.12	448.24	
4	217.23	18.47	235.70	
5	287.26	24.42	311.68	
6	322.42	27.41	349.83	
7	726.42	61.75	788.17	
8	114.22	9.71	123.93	2,257.55
10	108.24	9.22	117.46	
11	33.68	2.86	36.54	154.00
12	322.58	27.42	350.00	
13	522.12	44.38	566.50	
14	227.89	19.37	247.26	
15	67.42	5.73	73.15	1,236.91
17	587.24	49.92	637.16	
18	200.58	17.05	217.63	854.79
19	487.32	41.42	528.74	
20	128.54	10.93	139.47	
21	365.24	31.05	396.29	1,064.50
22	287.12	24.41	311.53	
24	198.47	16.87	215.34	.526.87
25	318.02	27.03	345.05	
26	77.21	6.56	83.77	
27	322.58	27.42	350.00	778.82
28	187.54	15.94	203.48	
29	118.29	10.06	128.35	
31	210.12	17.86	227.98	559.81
TOTALS	6,850.87	582.38	7,433.25	7,433.25

When the Browns close the books at the end of the year, the total of all monthly net sales will be used to calculate the annual income for the business. Remember that only net sales can be used to calculate income; the income tax collected must be set aside in a taxes payable account, so all taxes collected can be paid to the state at the end of the accounting period.

Annual Summary of Cash Receipts				
Month	Net Sales	Sales Tax	Daily Receipts	Deposits
January	$6,850.87	$582.38	$7,433.25	$7,433.25
February	$7,587.42	$489.34	$8,076.76	$8,076.76
March	$6,687.22	$568.41	$7,255.63	$7,255.63
April	$5,988.35	$509.01	$6,497.36	$6,497.36
Totals	xxx	xxx	xxx	xxx

- ## Journal of Business Expenses

The Browns use another journal to record all the business expenses that are paid using the business checking account. The Monthly Check Disbursement Journal has columns for the day of the month, the check number, the party to whom the check is payable, and the amount.

The additional columns allow the Browns to specify what the funds are being used to pay for. For example, check #126 to AT&T pays for the monthly phone bill, so the total amount is recorded in the Telephone column. Other expenses, like Checks 125 and 133 to the Browns' employee show the amount of the payment that is used for payroll tax. And Check #24 to Petty Cash shows that some of the money was used to pay for postage, with the balance used to restore the balance in the petty cash fund.

The total amount of all checks written can be included in the ledger; the additional columns that specify how the funds were used can help the Browns isolate specific expenses, revenue, and taxes payable when they close their books at the end of the accounting cycle.

The example below illustrates how a check disbursement journal can be set up. In addition, the information in this monthly journal can be transferred into the annual ledger, as in the example above.

Day	Payable To	Check #	Amount	Materials	Payroll	Payroll taxes	Electricity	Rent	Telephone	Transportation	Owner Salary	Other Expenses	
							Check Disbursement Journal						
							Year: 20	Month: January					
3	City Hall	123	$35.00									Buisness License	$35.00
4	ABC Marketing and Sales	124	$150.00									Advertisisng	$150.00
5	Margaret O'Sullivan	125	$205.00		$250.00	-$45.00							
6	AT&T	126	$28.95						$28.95				
7	Downtown Auto	127	$275.00	$125.00								Labor	$150.00
8	Alan Brown	128	$250.00								$250.00		
8	Mary Brown	129	$250.00								$250.00		
9													
10	Central Electric	130	$47.52				$47.52						
11													
12													
13													
14													
15													
16	ABC Gas	131	$47.52							$47.52			
17													
18	City Parking	132	$75.00							$75.00			
19	Margaret O'Sullivan	133	$205.00		$250.00	-$45.00							
20													
21													
22													
23													
24	Petty Cash	134	$45.00									Postage	$3.00
25													
26													
27													
28	Acme Property Management	135	$325.00					$325.00					
29													
30													
31	State Franchise Tax Board	136	$582.38									Sales tax	$582.38
	Bank Fee		$12.00										$12.00
Totals			$2,533.37	$125.00	$500.00	$0.00	$47.52	$325.00	$28.95	$122.52	$500.00		$932.38

Bank reconciliation statement

Finally, The Browns' single-entry cash accounting system will likely require them to reconcile their books with their bank statement each month to ensure there are no inaccurate entries. The Browns use the bank reconciliation form below to complete the following steps for this bookkeeping function, as follows:

1. Mary Brown enters the bank statement balance of $2,426.52.

2. Mary compares the deposits listed in the bank statement with the deposits shown in the checkbook. She sees that two deposits that appeared in the checkbook – one for $778.82 and another for $559.81 – did not appear on the bank statement. She enters the missing amounts on the bank reconciliation form and adds them to the bank statement balance. The subtotal is now $3,765.15.

3. Next, Mary compares all the canceled checks with the check register and locates three outstanding checks totaling $218.62. By subtracting this amount from the subtotal, she arrives at the adjusted balance of $3,546.53.

4. Now, Mary enters the checkbook balance showing in the company's business checkbook.

5.　　　　　　Mary locates an error that Alan made when he recorded a deposit of $683.42 that should have been $638.42. This is a difference of $45.00, which she subtracts from the checkbook balance. In addition, the bank service fee of $12.00 was not entered into the checkbook, so Mary deducts it here. The result is $3,546.53, which is the same amount listed in the adjusted balance in #3, above.

Bank Reconciliation

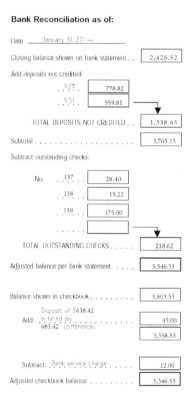

Bank Reconciliation as of:

Date _____ January 31, 20 —

Closing balance shown on bank statement. . | 2,426.52 |

Add deposits not credited:

　　　. 1/27 . | 778.82 |

　　　. 1/31 . | 559.81 |

　　TOTAL DEPOSITS NOT CREDITED . . | 1,338.63 |

Subtotal . . . . | 3,765.15 |

Subtract outstanding checks:

No. . 137 . . . | 28.40 |

. 138 . . | 15.22 |

. 139 . . | 175.00 |

. . . . . | |

TOTAL OUTSTANDING CHECKS . . . . . | 218.62 |

Adjusted balance per bank statement . . . . | 3,546.53 |

Balance shown in checkbook . . . . | 3,603.53 |

Deposit of $638.42
Add: entered as . . . . | 45.00 |
683.42 (difference)

| 3,558.53 |

Subtract: Bank service charge . . . . . | 12.00 |

Adjusted checkbook balance . . . . | 3,546.53 |

Chapter 8: How to Set Up a Double-Entry Bookkeeping System

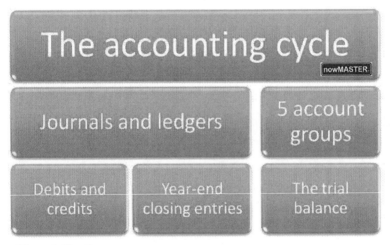

Figure 9: Free Image

The previous chapter illustrated how a small business owner can use a single-entry cash accounting system to record even a fairly complex array of transactions. Whether you are responsible for issuing payroll checks with tax deductions; loan payments; processing payments for sales of goods and services; or recording the daily costs associated with running your business, a well-designed single-entry cash accounting system can meet your needs.

Many people and businesses now use bookkeeping and accounting software. Bookkeeping and accounting software offers many advantages over paper-based bookkeeping systems. For example, most programs include error-checking functions and allow people with a limited knowledge of bookkeeping to jump right in without undergoing extensive training and certification. Bookkeeping programs also allow users to search for specific transactions that have been stored in the software's database and to create financial statements and reports fairly easily.

Bookkeeping software generally uses a double-entry system to record transactions. Although the software itself can make this more complex system of bookkeeping easier to manage, it's a good idea to have a basic understanding of how a double-entry system should be used to record business transactions. This section provides a step-by-step illustration of how to keep the books using a double-entry system.

Identifying and Classifying Accounting Source

Documents

No matter what type of business transaction you want to record in your bookkeeping system, that transaction must be associated with some type of documentation. Make sure you have set up a system in which you have control over the documents you produce and receive.

Depending on the type of transaction, many people may receive a copy of the accounting source document, which may vary in complexity. Documents may be electronic files such as PDF or Word documents; they may be electronically produced paper documents, such as computer receipts; or they may be written paper documents. Regardless of what form the document takes or what type of transaction it represents, you should first ensure that all your accounting source documents contain all the following information:

- the transaction date
- the amount of the transaction
- the names of the people or companies involved in the transaction
- some type of reference number
- a description of the transaction

In addition, your accounting source documents may result from any of the following types of transactions:

- quotes from sellers of inventory or supplies

- orders from customers or clients with the details of what they are requesting from your business.

- Delivery dockets or bills of lading that include a description of all items purchased, along with costs, quantities, totals, taxes, and any other related costs.

- Sales and purchase invoices and receipts. These documents are similar to dockets but are issued when a sale is made and include the details of the goods or services purchased; any terms of payment that may have been agreed to; and amounts owed and/or paid.

- Credit and debit notes. These receipts are issued either when a customer returns an item. The seller's receipt of the transaction shows a reduction in the amount owed by the customers, so it is called a credit note; the customer's receipt for this transaction shows a reduction in the amount they owe the seller, so it is called a credit note.

- Payment remittances are issued by customers when they pay their invoices; they are also issued by businesses to let customers know their payments have been received.

Recording Daily Transactions

During the day-to-day operation of your business, you will complete many transactions. As a result, you will produce and receive many accounting source documents. The double-entry bookkeeping process starts with transferring the information contained in the documents to the bookkeeping journal. Chapter 7 provides an illustration of a daily and monthly cash receipt journal. A company that uses double-entry bookkeeping will have to use a different approach to record these transactions.

Setting Up Journals

Double-entry bookkeeping will use two types of journals:
- General journals
- Special journals
  - Sales journals
  - Cash receipts journals
  - Sales return journals
  - Purchase journals

o   Cash payment journals

o   Purchase return journals

The general journal serves as a business's main bookkeeping journal. Most transactions should be recorded in the general ledger. Special journals allow for more efficient and easier recording of transactions of a similar type.

General Journal

We will begin by illustrating how to record transactions in a general journal. Using the example in Chapter 7, we will show how the Browns would record payment for their telephone bill on January 6, which appears in the Monthly Check Disbursement record in Chapter 7.

First, you will need to create a blank page for general journal entries, with five columns:

				J1
Date	**Description**	**Dr**	**Cr**	**Ref**
Jan 06, 20---	Telephone	28.95		003

			28.95	001
	Telephone bill paid with Ck #126			

In this example, the method of recording the same transaction is very different:

- At the top, the page journal is identified as J1.
- The first description shows "Telephone," and indicates that the Telephone account in the main ledger should be debited.
- The second line is indented and shows that the "Checking" account in the ledger should be credited for the same amount.
- The Ref column can serve two purposes:
  - By entering "P" in this column, the bookkeeper can indicate that the transaction has been posted to the ledger.
  - Alternatively, the numbers in the Ref account in this example indicate the ledger account number to which these transactions should be posted – the telephone account is

#003 in the Chart of Accounts; the Checking account is 001.

- The page number of the journal will be used as a reference in the ledger to show where the posted transaction is located in the journal.

- The next business transaction can be recorded directly beneath this transaction, after skipping one line in the journal.

Special Journals

To illustrate the difference between a general journal and special journal, let's first create a hypothetical transaction in a general journal that records a sale on credit. For example, using the Browns' computer repair business, let's say they sold a computer repair service to a walk-in customer. The customer needed the repair done immediately and agreed to send payment within 30 days of receiving the invoice. Here's how the record would look in the general journal:

				J2
Date	Description	Dr	Cr	Ref

Jan 12, 20---	Accounts Receivable	225.00		002
			225.00	004
	Mr. Adams: Pmt. in 30 days.			

Because it can be difficult to enter every credit sale in the general journal, then transfer everything to the general ledger, and then make adjustments when accounts payable are converted to revenue or income, it may be easier to create a special journal that records only credit sales. If all the transactions in such a special journal result from credit sales, the bookkeeper eliminates the need to enter debit, credit, and description information for every transaction. Instead, a special journal can be created to record shorthand versions of these transactions:

	SJ1

Date	Account	Inv. No.	Terms	Ref	Amount
Jan 06	B. Barnes	2001	30 days	B	180.00
Jan 12	A. Adams	2002	60 days	A	225.00
Jan 22	H. Franklin	2003	30 days	H	210.00
Jan 31	Dr Accounts Receivable, Cr. Sales				615.00

Thus, in this special journal to record only this type of transaction:

- The "Description" field is replaced with an "Account" field that contains the customer's name.
- "Invoice" and "Terms" fields replace the Dr and Cr fields.
- The "Reference" field now refers to the account holder's first initial, rather than the account in the ledger.
- Credits and Debits are indicated at the bottom of the journal on the last day of the month,

just before the information is transferred to the general journal and ledger.

Similar variations can be created for any type of specialized transaction that occurs frequently.

Transferring Journal Entries to the Ledger

Chapter 7 illustrated how the Browns' single-entry bookkeeping system tracked daily receipts and spending, then transferred the results to a monthly worksheet, and then transferred the monthly results to an annual summary. Double-entry systems are similar, but they require the bookkeeper to transfer all the general and special journal entries into the general ledger, also using debits and credits to record every transaction twice.

Remember that the Chart of Accounts lists all of a company's accounts – assets, liabilities, equity, expenses, and revenue. In addition, three types of ledgers are used to record business transactions:

- A general ledger
- An accounts payable ledger
- An accounts receivable ledger

The general ledger is the main ledger for bookkeeping. Each account from the chart of accounts is assigned its own page in the general ledger. Accounts with many transactions may use several pages, but in no case should transactions form more than one account appear on the same page of the general ledger.

Next, transactions from the General Journal should be transferred to the appropriate page of the General Ledger. The following example shows a page from the Checking account in the General Ledger of the Browns' business:

Checking							001
Date	Description	Ref	Debit	Date	Description	Ref	Credit
Jan 01	Opening balance		3750.00	Jan 03		J2	67.00
Jan 07		J1	225.00	Jan 06		J1	28.95
Jan 24		J2	72.50	Jan 14		J1	88.00

General ledgers in a double-entry system share many common features:

- Notice the "T-account" structure, with debits recorded on the left and credits recorded on the right.
- The Date columns indicate the month for which transactions are being recorded.
- The debt columns on the left increase the balance in the checking account, so this is where deposits are posted.
- The credits on the right decrease the checking balance, so this is where withdrawals are posted. (Notice the Browns' telephone bill from January 06).
- The References field shows the page number of the journal from which the information was taken.
- Descriptions are recorded in the journals, so there is less of a need to record them in the ledger.

At the end of the month, the bookkeeper totals the amounts of debits and credits. Credits are subtracted from debits to calculate the closing balance. That figure is used as the new opening balance for the next month.

Accounts Payable and Accounts Receivable Ledgers

These types of ledgers are similar to the special journals that help the bookkeeper record specific types of transactions during the month. Accounts Payable ledgers help the bookkeeper to keep track of how much money a business owes its creditors; the Accounts Receivable ledger help the bookkeeper to keep track of how much money clients and customers owe the business.

Although they are called Accounts Payable and Accounts Receivable ledger, they are subsidiary ledgers. They are not used themselves in creating reports or financial statements. Instead, the balances in these two types of lagers are transferred to the corresponding accounts in the General Ledger. Following are two examples of Accounts Receivable Ledgers taken from the examples above:

B Barnes					B
Date		Ref	Debit	Credit	Balance
Jan 06	Terms 30	SJ1	180.00		180.00

A Adams					A
Date		**Ref**	**Debit**	**Credit**	**Balance**
Jan 12	Terms 60	SJ1	225.00		225.00

Accounts Payable ledgers are structured similarly, with the following features:

- The customer or client name in the upper left of the page.
- The page name on the upper right.
- The Ref field references the special journal from which the information was taken.

Double-entry Bookkeeping Example

To illustrate how the double-entry bookkeeping system works in practice, let's create a simple example using the Browns' computer repair shop as the business for whom we are keeping books. We will illustrate using two types of transactions:

- an income transaction;
- an expense transaction.

Then, we will show how those transactions should be recorded using:

- a journal
- a ledger
- a report

- ## Income transaction

On January 15, Alan Brown opens Brown Computer Repair at 8:00am. At 8:30, his first customer of the day, Mr. Gates, walks in. His customer requests a tune-up and virus removal for his laptop. Alan Brown writes the invoice and tells the customer the job will be completed by 3:00pm that day. The total cost is $125.95. The customer pays cash using a debit card from his bank. Alan Brown places the receipt from the debit card transaction in the bookkeeping file in the back office.

- ## Expense transaction

On January 17, Alan Brown receives the monthly electric bill for Brown Computer Repair. The bill is for $37.26 and shows the date of the bill, the description of charges, and the amount. Alan writes check #226 to the local electrical utility provider. He places the check in the mail and puts the check receipt from the check register, along with a copy of the bill, in the bookkeeping file in the back office.

At the end of the week, the bookkeeper processes all business transactions for the week in the following order:

1.   enter transactions into journals;

| 2. | | post journal entire sot ledgers; |
| 3. | | create reports. |

- ## Journal entries

The bookkeeper's first task is to enter the transactions into the general journal. Journal entries are determined by the receipts and invoices and are entered chronologically, with a debit entry, a credit entry, and a description line. There should be a one-line space between entries. Here is how the journal entries looked for this week at Brown Computer repair:

				J1
Date	**Description**	**Dr**	**Cr**	**Ref**
Jan 15	Checking	125.95		
	Sales		125.95	

	Mr. Gates: Debit card pmt.			
Jan 17	Electric	37.26		
	Checking		37.26	
	January utility bill, Ck. #226			

- ## Posting to the Ledger

At the end of the month, the bookkeeper must post all the transactions recorded in the journal to the general ledger. There are two transactions to post for this example. The ledger is organized by account type, so the bookkeeper must identify which accounts in the general ledger he will have to access.

The income transaction shows a debit to the Checking account and a Credit to the Sales account. The expense transaction shows a debit to the Electricity account and a credit to the Checking account. So, the bookkeeper will have to post transactions to three different accounts in the ledger:

- Checking
- Sales
- Electricity

Here is how these three transactions look when the bookkeeper has completed posting them to the ledger:

Checking								001
Date	Description	Ref	Debit	Date	Description	Ref	Credit
Jan 01	Opening balance		3750.00	Jan 17		J1	37.26
Jan 15		J1	125.95				
Jan 31	Closing balance		88.69				

				Sales			002
Date	Descrip tion	Ref	Debi t	Date	Descrip tion	Ref	Credi t
Jan 01	Openin g balance		0.00	Jan 15	Mr. Gates: Debit purcha se	J1	125.9 5
				Jan 31	Closing balance		125.9 5

				Electricity			003
Date	Descrip tion	Ref	Debi t	Date	Descrip tion	Ref	Cred it

Jan 01	Openin g balance		00.0 0				
Jan 17	Monthl y bill	J1	37.2 6				
Jan 31	Closing balance		37.2 6				

- **Preparing reports**

Finally, the bookkeeper will prepare reports at the end of the accounting cycle. In this example, the bookkeeper will create a Balance sheet showing profit and loss. Obviously, this is a very simple example, but it illustrates how the accounting cycle progresses and how double-entry bookkeeping can make this process work:

Profit and Loss Statement

Income

Description	Amount
Cash sales	125.95

	Amount
Total Income	125.95

Cost of Goods Sold

Description	Amount

(eg stock, inventory, materials sold to customers or used to manufacture goods sold to customers)

	Amount
Total Cost of Sales	

	Amount
Gross Profit	125.95

(Total Income less Cost of Sales)

Expenses

Description	Amount

(example - Advertising, Stationery, Postage, Fuel)

Electricity	37.26

	Amount
Total Expenses	37.26

	Amount
Net Profit	88.69

(Gross Profit less Expenses)

Chapter 9: Accounting Systems:

Principles

The first eight chapters of this book have explored the fundamentals of bookkeeping. These chapters have discussed the two types of bookkeeping systems – single-entry and double-entry; the two types of accounting methods – cash and accrual; the accounting and bookkeeping cycle from collecting records of business transactions, to recording transactions in a journal, to posting them in a ledger, to creating financial statements at the end of the accounting and bookkeeping cycle. Clearly, every business may face a multitude of varying challenges on any given day, so it is not possible to foresee every possibility you may encounter in your efforts in professional bookkeeping. However, the previous chapters have mentioned one concern that deserves additional attention.

The main function of bookkeeping is to allow business owners to formulate an accurate assessment of their business's overall financial condition and performance. This chapter explores some of the ways well-designed financial statements can help business owners, investors, and financial regulators accurately assess the current state of financial health of any given business, as well as its potential for increased profitability and growth.

Figure 10: Free Image

Knowing How to Run Your Business

Running a business effectively requires a broad range of knowledge and access to resources. Perhaps most important, the business owner must understand the value of the goods and services his or her business will be providing, and how to produce and deliver high-quality products and services. Consider the vast array of products and services that are available in both local and global markets:

- Consumer retail businesses such as department stores

- Hotels and restaurants
- Automobile dealerships and repair services
- Grocery stores
- Hobbies and other specialized interests, such as camping and outdoor living; musical instrument sales and instruction; pet supply stores, etc.
- Real estate and investing firms
- Legal and other professional service firms
- Advertising, sales, and marketing
- Technology supplies and service

The list is virtually endless. Each sector of business requires extensive knowledge not only of the specifics of the types of goods and services a given area of business should be able to provide, but also more general business knowledge, including advertising; personnel management; lead generation; occupational safety and health; public relations; and much more.

But regardless of the specific nature and the day-to-day details of operating your business, all businesses share one common aspect: bookkeeping is an essential daily function. It is true that providing quality goods and services that answer a genuine need or desire will always be one of the key aspects of success in the professional world. However, even a business that offers the highest quality goods and services can suffer and fail financially if they do not employ effective financial management tools.

Gaining Knowledge of a Business Through

Bookkeeping

The three main types of financial statements – the balance sheet; the income statement; and the cash flow statement – each provide unique opportunities for gaining knowledge about any given business's core functions, profitability, competitiveness, and potential of further growth. Furthermore, the reason these three types of reports have been identified as the standard for financial statements that comply with Generally Accept Accounting Principles (GAAP) is because each type of report allows for the assessment of a different aspect of the business's performance. Together, all three allow for complete knowledge of the business's operations.

Many people may be interested in analyzing financial performance records to gain knowledge of a business. For example, the following occupational groups routinely seek to know businesses through a deep understanding of their business operations:

- **Creditors**. Any financial services organization that issues business loans will ask questions to determine whether the company has the capacity to repay. Often, they will request cash flow statements, so they can determine whether a company exercises appropriate discipline in the regulation of its expenses and income.

- **Investors**. If you work for or own a company that issues shares or is managed by investment partners, these individuals will be interested in examining financial statements for evidence that the company will be able to continue paying dividends to existing investors, or whether the company may be an attractive opportunity for future investors.

- **Management**. The goal of business management is to ensure that the company maintains operational efficiency and profitability. While ensuring that the needs of personnel and facilities are addressed is a very important aspect of management, no management team can assess whether their efforts are successful without examining the financial statements at the end of each accounting cycle.

- **Financial regulators**. Publicly held companies are required to submit financial statements to the Securities and Exchange Commission (SEC) to ensure GAAP compliance. In addition, any business may be audited by the IRS, and financial statements will be the main source of information.

Those interested in gaining knowledge of any business may choose to focus on one type of report over another depending upon their concerns. Specifically, each of the three types of reports may offer the following types of insights:

- **Balance sheets**: These reports can help investors and regulators determine such factors as asset turnover, receivables turnover, debt-to-asset ratios, and debt-to-equity ratios. Thus, the balance sheet provides a means to gain knowledge of a company's essential value at a given point in time.

- **Income statements**: These reports help investors and regulators determine a given company's gross profit margin, net profit margin, ratio of tax efficiency, and interest coverage.

- **Cash flow statements**: These reports help investors and regulators assess a company's ability to generate cash-driven revenue by showing the relationship between cash and overall earnings before interest, taxes, depreciation, and amortization. Thus, simply because a company can report a net profit at the end of the year does not necessarily mean that they have been successful in selling goods and services – this report can help determine whether profitability resulted instead from non-operating activity, such as loans or investments.

Analyzing Financial Reports

This section examines the specific types of financial analysis, as well as an overview of processes commonly employed to gain knowledge of businesses by examining their financial records.

Essentially, there are two types of financial analysis:

- Horizontal and vertical analysis
- Ratio analysis

Horizontal and Vertical Analysis

This type of financial analysis is typically used to analyze the results of income statements.

First, horizontal analysis compares the performance of certain aspect of a business's financial performance over two or more accounting periods. A horizontal analysis of any business may compare the change from one year to the next of a single aspect of its balance sheet – for example, a company's gross profits from sales. This analysis of the year-over-year (YoY) change in any given line item of a financial statement uses a specific formula:

Percentage of Change= (Value of Period N)/(Value of Period N-1)-1.

For example, let's calculate the YoY change in gross profits between 2017 and 2016 for Company ABC:

- In 2017, the company generated $4,000 gross profit in sales.
- In 2016, gross profit from sales was $3,000.
- YoY change is calculated as follows:
  - Percentage of YoY change = ($4,000 / $3,000) − 1
  - Percentage of YoY change = 1.33 − 1
  - Percentage of YoY change = .33
  - YoY change = 33%

Next, vertical analysis compares the line items of any given financial report within one single year to understand the significance of the relationships among the various statistics for that reporting year. For this example, we will consider the income statement for Company ABC. In the following illustration, you can see on the left the breakdown of the company's income; on the right, you can see an analysis of those numbers that shows the percentage of each figure in relation to revenue:

Company ABC Income Statement		
	2018	**2018**
Revenue	500,000	100%
COGS	(300,200)	-64%
Gross Profit	**100,800**	**36%**
Depreciation	(500,000)	-10%
SG&A	(300,000)	-6%
Interest	(5,000)	-1%
Earnings before tax	**95,000**	**19%**
Tax	(22,500)	-5%

Net earnings	72,500	15%

Because this type of analysis compares statistical reporting data within one vertical column of figures, it is referred to as vertical analysis.

Ratio Analysis

Ratio analysis takes a different approach. Ratio analysis calculates the relative size or value of one statistic to another. This ratio is then used as a standard of comparison to determine how a company is performing – either in relation to a prior time period or to an industry standard. Generally, ration analysis should confirm expectations, but it can also indicate areas of concerns. There are several main categories of ratio analysis:

- Liquidity ratios measure the ability of a business to remain in operation by examining the following factors:
  - Cash coverage ratios comparing available cash to pay interest;
  - Current ratios measuring amount of liquid assets available to pay liabilities;

- o   Quick ratios, which are the same as current ratios, except that they exclude inventory;
- o   Liquidity index, which measures how long it will take to convert assets to cash.
- Activity ratios show how well a company is managing the use of its resources and include:
  - o   Accounts payable turnover ratios
  - o   Accounts receivable turnover ratios
  - o   Fixed asset turnover ratio
  - o   Inventory turnover ratio
  - o   Sales to working capital ratio
  - o   Working capital turnover ratio
- Leverage ratios measure the degree to which a company is relying on debt to maintain operations and includes the following:
  - o   Debt-to-equity ratio
  - o   Debt service coverage ratio
  - o   Fixed charge coverage ratio
- Profitability ratios measure the ability of a company to generate profit and include:
  - o   Break-even point ratio
  - o   Contribution margin ratio
  - o   Gross profit ratio
  - o   Margin of safety

- ○   Net profit ratio
- ○   Return on equity ratio
- ○   Return on net assets ratio
- ○   Return on operating assets ratio

Decision Making Through Effective

Bookkeeping

Thus, there are two sides to effectively managing any type of business. Producing quality goods and services, selling them at competitive rates and prices, and ensuring that people are aware of your business are absolute essentials. Without these skills, no one would have any business to manage. It may be tempting to assume that you can make effective business decisions based exclusively on your expertise in your given field of professional work or your skill as a personnel manager. However, to make your business stand out and reach its full potential, you must harness the power of effective bookkeeping to gain insights into the ways your business operations can remain competitive.

The following six steps of the financial analysis process explain how a thorough understanding of the bookkeeping and accounting cycle can help you be a better business owner, or help you be a better bookkeeper for the business owners you serve:

1. Analyze the economics of the industry in which you are working.

Although GAAP-compliant bookkeeping and accounting methods apply across all industry lines, each industry will have its own particular characteristics. What types of goods or services does your industry produce? What is the industry standard method of producing and distributing these goods and services? Identifying the costs involved in these methods is known as a "value chain analysis," and you will be at a competitive disadvantage until you have a thorough understanding of your industry.

2. Establish a competitive strategy.

Consider the type of product or service your company offers. Is your product or service unique? What are your profit margins and access to other forms of capital? What about brand recognition? Have you assessed the demographic in which you will be offering goods and services? What strategy can you implement that will address all of these concerns?

3. Examine the financial statements.

Now that you have identified a specific business objective and a plan for achieving that objective, you can approach an analysis of the company's financial statements form an educated perspective. For each of the three types of reports, consider the following:

- Balance sheet: Does the company have sufficient assets to continue operating?
- Income statement: How successful is the company at generating revenue from sales of goods and services?
- Cash flow statement: Does the company exercise good judgment in managing its funds?

4. Conduct a thorough financial analysis.

Using the techniques of horizontal, vertical, and ratio analysis discussed earlier in this chapter, conduct a complete analysis of the company's performance. Focus specifically on areas you may have identified in the previous steps as needing improvement. How profitable is the company? Has performance been improving or declining? What does a financial analysis tell you about the areas that require greater attention?

5. Make recommendations

As the company's bookkeeper, you are in a unique position to contribute to a discussion of the direction of the company's direction for future growth and investment. Although market research and an assessment of the quality of the goods and services your company provides is a necessary part of this conversation, the hard date derived from a disciplined analysis of well-maintained and reliable accounting and bookkeeping records can provide invaluable insight.

6. Issue an official valuation of the company.

Especially if you are part of a publicly traded company, an annual statement that places a total value on the company can be the most important driver of success. If you are required to submit reports to the SEC, it is imperative that you show documentation of the reliability of your calculations. If you are a smaller, privately held company, a disciplined valuation can still allow you to benefit by appearing to be a more attractive investment to lenders, clients, and customers.

Chapter 10: QuickBooks

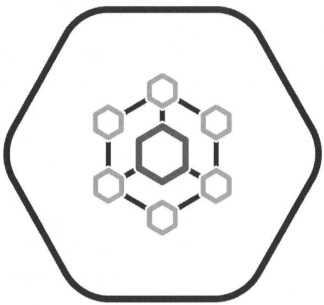

Figure 11: Free Image

A basic search using an internet search engine and the search term, "bookkeeping software," returns millions of results. There are over well over 20 recognized, well-known software applications that help business owners with a variety of bookkeeping and software tasks. Some of these services are available as software downloads and function as offline desktop applications that simply automate many bookkeeping and accounting chores. Others are available for purchases in office supply stores and offer similar features. Still others are designed as web-based applications that require an internet connection so that data can be stored in an off-site server. Web-based bookkeeping applications have become the most prominent type of bookkeeping software. Most of them require users to pay a monthly fee – usually about $10 per month for the most basic level of service. Among these types of automated bookkeeping software applications, some companies offer considerably more expensive versions that include the services of a human bookkeeping and accounting staff employed by the software company.

By far the most well-known of all these automated bookkeeping applications is QuickBooks, which was developed by Intuit Corporation. QuickBooks routinely receives the highest ratings of all major bookkeeping and accounting software applications and is generally considered the standard for the industry. Intuit, along with many independent, third-party companies have made available on the internet a vast selection of training videos and tutorials to help business owners learn how to navigate this powerful bookkeeping software. This chapter will cover some of the more basic functions to help you understand how software can help you make the bookkeeping process more efficient and reliable.

What Is QuickBooks? Why Should I Use It?

QuickBooks is accounting software designed to serve the needs of small- and medium-sized businesses. QuickBooks offers both desktop accounting applications and cloud- and web-based applications. QuickBooks is adaptable to most accounting and bookkeeping environments and includes many features, such as accepting and processing of payment for business services; payment and management of bills; customer and client invoicing; and employee payroll processing.

Although initial versions of the software did not accommodate double-entry accounting methods, it became very popular very quickly with many small business owners who had no formal training in bookkeeping and accounting. Subsequent updates have allowed QuickBooks to address many of the shortcomings of its earlier releases.

Beginning in 2000, QuickBooks was available in two versions – Basic and Pro. In 2002, an Enterprise version was released for medium-sized businesses. As of 2003, QuickBooks has released customized versions with specific functions and workflows designed specifically to meet the needs of differing types of businesses, such as manufacturing, wholesale, professional service firms, retailers, and non-profit organizations. There is even a version specifically designed for professional accountants that is capable of addressing all GAAP-required functions, such as creating audit trails and generating highly detailed professional financial statements. Over 50,000 accounting firms are members of the QuickBooks ProAdvisor program, and as of 2008, almost 95% of the bookkeeping software market was dominated by QuickBooks. The most recent versions of QuickBooks included updates that enable batch transactions, bill tracking, automated reports, smart search, and improved report filters.

QuickBooks Online

Figure 12: Free Image

QuickBooks offers an online web-based service called QuickBooks Online. To use this service, the user must register and pay a monthly fee. QuickBooks Online provides access to software functions through the internet instead of directly on the user's computer.

QuickBooks Online is a different product than the original QuickBooks accounting software. The online version includes ongoing updates and patches, but also includes pop-ads for upgrade services. Like the desktop application, QuickBooks Online is also the industry leader among web-based accounting applications. However, there are many products and services that offer greater competition to QuickBooks Online than to the desktop version.

QuickBooks Online is accessible through all major browsers and through all major devices, including mobile devices using Android or iOS operating systems. QuickBooks Online received a major redesign in 2013 and now allows for customization and integration with other third-party software and the proprietary applications of financial services companies such as banks and payroll management companies.

Setting Up a QuickBooks Inventory

There are thousands of tutorials and videos available online on the Intuit website as well as many third-party education and training sites. These videos and tutorials range from one-session how-to lessons about a specific function in QuickBooks all the way to complete training and certification courses designed for use by human resources departments. There are far too many possible bookkeeping scenarios involving far too much complexity to provide complete, detailed illustrations in this book. However, we have included below a brief overview of how to set up an inventory using QuickBooks to illustrate the usefulness of this bookkeeping and accounting software.

Note: The Inventory function described in this section is only available using a Plus-level subscription to QuickBooks Online.

1. **Sales** settings

    a. Click on the **Gear** icon in the upper right corner of the **Home Page**.

    b. Select **Accounts and Settings** from the dropdown menu.

    The **Accounts and Settings** page will appear on the screen.

c.   From the **Accounts and Settings** page, click Sales at the left of the screen.

d.   In the **Sales** window confirm that **"Track quantity and price/rate"** and **"Track inventory quantity on hand"** are set to **On**.

e.   Click the "x" in the upper-right corner to close the window.

2.   **Products and Services** settings

a.   Click on the **Gear** icon in the upper right corner of the **Home Page.**

b.   Select **Products and Services** from the drop-down menu.

The **Products and Services** page will appear on the screen.

c.   Create product categories:

i.   Select **Manage Categories** in the upper-left corner.

The **Product Categories** page will appear.

ii.   Click **New Category** in the upper-left corner.

iii.   Enter a name for the category in the **Name** field.

iv.   Click **Save**.

d.   Create sub-categories.

i.   Select **Manage Categories** in the upper-left corner.

The **Product Categories** page will appear.

ii.   Click **New Category** in the upper-left corner.

iii.   Enter a name for the sub-category in the **Name** field.

iv.   Check the "**Is a sub-category**" box beneath the **Name** field.

v.   Select the parent category from the drop-down menu beneath the **Name** field.

vi.   Click **Save**.

e.   Add products manually

i.   From the **Products and Services** page, click **New**.

ii.   Select an **Inventory Item**.

The item detail pane will appear.

iii.   Add as many details about the item as you would like, such as name, number, quantity, etc. There is also a space to add a picture.

iv.   Click **Save**.

f.   Alternatively, you can import product lists from an Excel spreadsheet.

i.   Form the **Products and Services** page, click the arrow next to **New**.

ii.   Click **Import**.

iii.   Click **Download a Sample File** to see how to format your existing spreadsheet.

iv.   After you have formatted your spreadsheet, click **Browse**.

v.   Select the appropriate file from your computer and follow the on-screen instructions.

g.   Create a purchase order to buy inventory.

i.   From the **Home Page,** click the **Plus Sign**.

ii.   Click **Purchase Order**.

A purchase order form will appear.

iii.   Complete the details in the **Purchase Order** form.

iv.   Click **Save and send**.

The purchase order will be sent to your supplier.

h.   Create a bill for the purchase order

i.   From the **Home Page**, choose **Transactions** on the left menu.

ii.   Choose **Expenses**.

iii.   Select the purchase order you created in (i).

iv.   Click the arrow to the right of the **Send** button.

A drop-down menu appears.

v.   Click **Copy to bill.**

A bill will be generated for the purchase order.

vi.   Check the details.

vii.   Click **Save and send**.

i.   Generate an invoice for customer sales.

    i.   From the **Home Page,** click the **Plus Sign.**

    ii.   Click **Invoice**.

An invoice form will appear.

    iii.   Complete the details.

    iv.   Click **Save and Send**.

Inventory quantities will be automatically adjusted, and the customer will receive an invoice.

j.   Adjust Inventory manually.

    i.   Click on the **Gear** icon in the upper right corner of the **Home Page.**

    ii.   Select **Products and Services** from the drop-down menu.

The **Products and Services** page will appear on the screen.

iii.   Locate the item whose quantity you want to adjust.

iv.   Click on the arrow next to the **Edit** button.

v.   Click **Adjust Quantity.**

The **Inventory Quantity Adjustment** window appears.

vi.   Click in the **New QTY** box and enter the new quantity.

vii.   Click **Save and send**.

k.   View Inventory Reports.

i.   From the **Home Page**, choose **Reports** on the left menu.

The Reports page appears.

ii.   Click **All Reports**.

The **All Reports** page appears.

iii.   Choose **Manage Products and Inventory**.

iv.   The **Manage Products and Inventory** window appears.

v.   Click **Sales by Product/Service Summary**. (You may also view the **Inventory Valuation Summary** or any of the other available reports.)

The **Sales by Product/Service Summary** report appears.

Chapter 11: Adapting the Basics of Bookkeeping to Different Businesses

By now, you have absorbed the basic fundamentals of bookkeeping and accounting; their importance to running a business successfully; and the many options available to all business owners interested in streamlining their operations. This chapter will address one final concern. As the examples in the previous chapters have illustrated, the size, complexity, and type of any given business is one of the most important considerations when deciding which type of bookkeeping and accounting methods are most appropriate. So, in this chapter, we will explore specifically how bookkeeping methods can be adapted to ensure the needs and demands of any business are best served. Specifically, this chapter explores how the bookkeeping priorities may differ among three types of businesses:

- retail sales and/or restaurants;
- real estate companies;
- personal and/or professional service companies.

Retail and Restaurants

For most of us, a business is a place where we go to do our shopping, pay for essential services, or spend time in leisure activities. We have all grown comfortable with the idea of huge multinational corporations with billion-dollar budgets and global offices equipped with satellite communication. Many of us are employed by such organizations, and if you are reading this book, you may work in the bookkeeping and accounting department of large corporations. On the other hand, the bookkeeping needs of smaller, local businesses are vastly different than the concerns of global competition faced by Wall Street corporations. Let's examine how a smaller retail business or restaurant can optimize its bookkeeping:

Inventory

If you operate a retail business, your inventory is the most important asset. In fact, of all your investments, inventory may represent the largest percentage. As a result, your inventory tracking system should reflect the importance of this aspect of your business. Here's what your bookkeeping records should record:

- Daily changes to inventory quantities resulting from shipments received and customer sales.
- Quantities and costs of all shipments received, and all products sold.
- Regular adjustments to account for lost, stolen, or damaged items.

If you are keeping the books for a restaurant, you should also keep track of the following concerns:

- Changes in daily food inventory, including dates and lists of every item purchased.
- Daily food sales, including the number of meals served during each meal period of the day.
- Location where meals were served.
- Revenues associated with meal sales.
- Beverage sales, including types of beverages, quantities, times sold, and revenue earned.

Income

All sources of income should be recorded. Obviously, in retail sales, sales should be the main source of revenue, and your records should be as detailed as possible. But there are other sources of income that should be recorded as well, such as after-sale service fees. You will also want to set up a system to conduct regular audits of point-of-sale machinery to ensure there are no inaccuracies.

If you are keeping books for a restaurant, you should also consider a system that allows each cash register to record individual sales, as well as cash transactions conducted by servers, including taxes, tips, and payments by credit card.

Expenses

Regardless of the type of retail business you run, you should automate as many payment expenses as you can, such as utilities, rent and lease payments, and any other regularly occurring payments. Expenses also include employees' wages and payroll taxes, so you should set up an entirely separate bookkeeping system to ensure compliance with all applicable laws. Make sure you also provide a space for insurance, marketing, administrative expenses, depreciation, loan payments, startup costs, and anticipated repairs and maintenance costs.

Accounts Payable and Receivable

Be sure to keep detailed records of all the money you owe and all the money that is owed to you. If you use automated bookkeeping software, set up reminders for loan payments, bills, and credit debts, as well as to guide collections activities for credit customers. These bookkeeping items are crucial to a small store or restaurant and managing your payables and receivables effectively can boost your credit rating and help you maintain a positive cash flow.

Retained Earnings

You're in business for a reason: to come out ahead financially. Make sure all of your bookkeeping and accounting is designed to help you find ways to save money, increase profitability and efficiency, and monitor the growth of your re-investment.

Real Estate

Like retail businesses and restaurants, real estate companies should have a system that records income and expenses. But real estate investment is an entirely different type of business venture that requires adaptations of the bookkeeping system:

- Inventory. For a real estate investor, the inventory is the prospective homes and buildings he or she may either sell or purchase for profit. These are not simple inventory items that need to be accounted for merely by tracking quantities and costs. The real estate investment business is complex, and your inventory is your main concern. Your bookkeeping system needs to be able to track the multitude of factors that are used to determine competitive market prices.

- Business metrics. As a real estate investor, your financial concerns extend beyond your own personal investment goals and the soundness of your company's finances. Having readily available data and analytics to help you understand the financial backgrounds of your clients, customers, and the real estate market generally will make the determination of whether your real estate investment firm is successful. Ensure your bookkeeping system can account for all of the following factors:

- ○ Job performance across your entire network.
- ○ Tax preparedness
- ○ Cash flow awareness
- ○ Credit score management

Personal and Professional Service Firms

Finally, professional service companies may have unique concerns because unlike retail stores, restaurants, and real estate firms, they are not selling any tangible items. Because this business model is radically different from retail consumer sales, the bookkeeping systems should be able to address a different set of concerns as well.

To begin, professional service firms will have less of a concern about initiating inventory records. Professional service firms may offer a wide variety of professional services:

- Legal services

- Medical services
- Counseling service
- Tax filing services
- Consulting in a variety of areas.

Because of the potential for malpractice and other types of litigation, the success of a professional service firm may be more heavily dependent on the firm's sound financial foundation. Here are some of the considerations commonly addressed by the accounting systems of professional service firms:

- monthly costs like billable hours, travel, and marketing.
- client billing systems that incorporate medical insurance billing or other types of compensation.
- cash flow statements and commission tracking reports to determine whether your practice is profitable.
- continuing education, training, certification, and accreditation.

Every business will have unique challenges and concerns. However, bookkeeping and accounting methods and systems have been firmly established across all areas of business. No matter how big or small, or how simple or complex your business model, a well-designed bookkeeping and accounting system can help you operate more efficiently, profitably, and effectively.

Chapter 12: Glossary

Common Terms Used in Bookkeeping and

Accounting

Account: A space in a ledger reserved for recording all the transactions of a specific type. For example, all sales transactions will be recorded in the Sales account.

Accounting: the practice of entering bookkeeping records into a ledger and producing financial statements.

Accounting Equation: the accounting equation is Assets = Liabilities + Owners' Equity. It is used to ensure that all records in a double-entry accounting system are balanced.

Accountant: the person responsible for processing and evaluating bookkeeping records. Sometimes used interchangeably with "bookkeeper."

Accounts Payable (A/P): all invoices and other expanse that a business has not yet paid.

Accounts Receivable (A/R): all revenue owed to a company that has not yet been paid.

Accrual Accounting: an accounting method in which income and expenses are recognized at the time they are incurred, instead of at the time they are paid.

Assets: all items of value that a company owns.

Bad Debts: sales invoices that have not been paid by customers, and that the company has written off as an expense.

Balance Sheet: one of three reports that comprise financial statements. The balance sheet provides information about a company's value by showing its assets, liabilities, and equity at a given point in time. The other two reports are the income statement and the cash flow statement.

Billing: the practice of sending invoices to clients and customers for goods sold or services rendered.

Bookkeeper: a person trained and experienced in recording all the daily transactions of a business in journals and ledgers. Sometimes used interchangeably with "accountant."

Bookkeeping: the professional practice of recording business transactions in journals and ledgers according to Generally Accepted Accounting Principles (GAAP).

Bookkeeping Cycle: a complete cycle of recording transactions before the records are transferred to the ledger and balanced. Usually a bookkeeping cycle is one month.

Budget: a fixed sum of money within which a household or business must function.

Capital: generally, funds or other forms of assets invested into a business to enable operations.

Cash Accounting: a method of accounting in which income and expenses are recorded when they are paid, instead of when they are incurred.

Cash Book: the main record of financial transactions for a business.

Cash Flow: the movement or "flow" of cash through a business. A cash flow statement can show how the business owner manages the money the business generates through operations.

Chart of Accounts: a list of all accounts contained in a company's ledger. The main account categories are assets, Liabilities, Equity, Revenue, Cost of Goods Sold, and Expenses. Each category may contain several accounts that record specific types of transactions.

Closing Balance: the final balance on a bank statement or cash book register at the end of a business day or bookkeeping cycle.

Coding: the practice of assigning transaction amounts to accounts in the chart of accounts.

Contra: contra accounts allow bookkeepers to counterbalance an entry into a ledger account. The Allowance for Bad Debts account is a contra account to the Sales Revenue account.

Cost of Goods Sold: the amount of money a company pays for items they purchase wholesale and then sale at retail for a profit. This can also refer to the costs of raw materials to manufacture products for resale.

Credit: bookkeeping entries that are entered on the right side of a double-entry bookkeeping ledger. Credits increase the value of income, liability, and equity accounts and decrease the value of asset and expense accounts.

Credit Note: a receipt for money refunded to a customer who was overcharged or who returned an item.

Creditor: a person or business who lends money or extends credit.

Data: information stored in journals and ledgers.

Debit: bookkeeping entries that are entered on the left side of a double-entry bookkeeping ledger. Debits decrease the value of income, liability, and equity accounts and increase the value of asset and expense accounts.

Debtor: a person or business who borrows money.

Deductible: a purchase that can be claimed as a business expense.

Deposit: money paid into a bank account.

Deposit Slip: a receipt showing the date amount of a deposit.

Depreciation: the amount of value an asset loses due to wear and tear.

Description: the section of a financial transaction record that provides information about the customer and the item purchased.

Docket: a document that provides information about a shipment of items purchased.

Double-Entry: double-entry bookkeeping requires two entries for every transaction – a debit entry and a credit entry. Debit entries must always equal credit entries for every transaction.

Drawings: the owners' salary.

End of Month: the process that occurs each month when the bookkeeper completes the bookkeeping cycle.

Entry/Entries: refers to all recorded financial transactions.

Equity: the difference between a company's assets and its liabilities.

Expense: purchases made to support a company's operations.

Financial Statements: reports of financial activities that allow businesses, investors, and regulators to determine the financial health of a company. They include the balance sheet, income statement, and the cash flow statement.

Fiscal Year: twelve consecutive months that constitute an entire accounting and bookkeeping cycle. A fiscal year can begin in any calendar month.

Funds: all of the money involved in all of a business's transactions.

Gross Profit: total business income less the cost of goods sold.

Income: money earned by a business through sales of goods and services.

Inventory: all the items that a company keeps on its premises available for sale.

Invoice: a document that shows the details of a purchase, including the goods or services purchased, the date, and the amount owed.

Journal: a chronological record of daily business transactions.

Ledger: a permanent record of daily business transactions organized by account type. The information in the ledger is taken from the journal.

Liability: debts that accompany owes.

Loan: a sum of money extended to a company or person that must be repaid, usually with interest.

Loss: Loss occurs when expenses are greater than income. The opposite of profit.

Net Profit: the result of subtracting the cost of expenses from gross profit.

Nil: a balance of zero.

Opening Balance: the balance of a financial account on the first day of a financial period.

Payable: a bill that is due to be paid by a business to a customer that has not yet been paid.

Payroll: the financial account from which funds are distributed to employees.

Petty Cash: a financial account that consists of a small amount of physical cash, so businesses can make minor purchases.

Profit: the difference between income and expenses.

Purchase: buying goods or services.

Quote: an estimate of the cost of goods or services.

Receipt: a document issued by a business to a customer showing the details of a sale of goods or services.

Receivable: accounts that are due to be paid to a business that have not yet been paid by the customer.

Reconcile: matching the calculations or balances from one document to another, as when someone reconciles their checkbook balance with their bank statement.

Recurring: a transaction that takes place repeatedly, at a regular time interval, such as a monthly utility bill.

Refund: money that is given back to the customer or a business after a purchase as a result of a dispute, an overpayment, or some other reason.

Reimburse: payment in return for some type of loss

Salary: a fixed amount of money paid to an employee for an agreed period of employment.

Sales: money received for goods or service purchased by customers.

Single-Entry: a bookkeeping method in which all financial transactions are only listed once.

Software: computer programs like QuickBooks that automate certain clerical or other tasks.

Statement: reports that display financial information, such as bank statements, or financial statements).

Transaction: a transfer of funds as a result of a sale or purchase.

Transfer: movement of funds from one account to another, usually for accounting purposes.

Undeposited Funds: an asset account showing funds that have not yet been deposited into the bank.

Unpresented: checks that have been written, sent, and received, but not yet deposited.

Withdrawal: money taken out of a financial account.

Write-Off: an amount of money owed that will not be paid.

Year-End: the financial accounting and bookkeeping activities that occur at the end of a fiscal year.

Resources

6 Steps to an Effective Financial Statement Analysis. (n.d.). Retrieved from https://www.afponline.org/ideas-inspiration/topics/articles/Details/6-steps-to-an-effective-financial-statement-analysis.

A guide to retail accounting. (n.d.). Retrieved from https://www.business.com/articles/jill-bowers-retail-accounting/

A Relatively Painless Guide to Double-Entry Accounting: Bench Accounting. (n.d.). Retrieved from https://bench.co/blog/accounting/double-entry-accounting

About Publication 583, Starting a Business and Keeping Records. (n.d.). Retrieved from https://www.irs.gov/forms-pubs/about-publication-583.

Account Types. (n.d.). Retrieved from https://www.principlesofaccounting.com/account-types/.

Accounting Basics: Debits and Credits. (2019, September 11). Retrieved from https://www.patriotsoftware.com/accounting/training/blog/debits-and-credits/.

Accounting for Contractors: Software, Billing & Taxes. (2016, October 19). Retrieved from https://www.homeadvisor.com/r/new-contractor-accounting-basics.

Accounts, Debits, and Credits. (n.d.). Retrieved from https://www.principlesofaccounting.com/chapter-2/accounts-debits-and-credits/.

Adamson-Pickett, J. (2019, October 11). Small Business Bookkeeping Basics. Retrieved from https://www.business.org/finance/accounting/small-business-bookkeeping-basics.

Albarado, L. M., Norman, A., Afzaal, M., Payne, P., Shelton, C., & Khlynovskiy, R. (2019, March 6). 39 Free QuickBooks Online Tutorials: Learn QuickBooks Fast. Retrieved from https://fitsmallbusiness.com/free-quickbooks-online-tutorials/.

Analysis of Financial Statements - Free Financial Analysis Guide. (n.d.). Retrieved from https://corporatefinanceinstitute.com/resources/knowledge/finance/analysis-of-financial-statements/.

Articles. (n.d.). Retrieved from https://www.afponline.org/ideas-inspiration/topics/articles/Details/6-steps-to-an-effective-financial-statement-analysis.

Balance Sheet Template for Excel. (n.d.). Retrieved from https://www.vertex42.com/ExcelTemplates/cash-flow-statement.html.

Beginners Guide to Financial Statement. (2007, February 5). Retrieved from https://www.sec.gov/reportspubs/investor-publications/investorpubsbegfinstmtguidehtm.html.

Bhosale, T., & *, N. (2019, October 9). General Journal vs General Ledger: Top 5 Differences (with Infographics). Retrieved from https://www.wallstreetmojo.com/general-journal-vs-general-ledger/.

Bookkeeping, S. L. C. (n.d.). Personal Tax Services. Retrieved from https://www.slcbookkeeping.com/personal-tax-services.

Bookkeeping - Double-Entry, Debits and Credits: AccountingCoach. (n.d.). Retrieved from https://www.accountingcoach.com/bookkeeping/explanation/3.

Bookkeeping Basics - Steps for Business Startups. (n.d.). Retrieved from https://www.beginner-bookkeeping.com/bookkeeping-basics.html.

Bookkeeping Basics: A How-To Guide for Small Business Owners: Bench Accounting. (n.d.). Retrieved from https://bench.co/bookkeeping-basics/.

Bookkeeping for Business: What You Need to Know. (n.d.). Retrieved from https://www.fundera.com/business-accounting/small-business-bookkeeping.

Bookkeeping Terms and Basic Accounting Definitions. (n.d.). Retrieved from https://www.beginner-bookkeeping.com/bookkeeping-terms.html.

Botkeeper. (n.d.). Bookkeeping for Professional Services. Retrieved from https://www.botkeeper.com/bookkeeping-for-professional-services.

Bragg, S. (2018, November 28). Financial statements. Retrieved from https://www.accountingtools.com/articles/2017/5/10/financial-statements.

Bragg, S. (2019, August 17). Debits and credits. Retrieved from https://www.accountingtools.com/articles/2017/5/17/debits-and-credits.

Bragg, S. (2019, April 10). The difference between a journal and a ledger. Retrieved from https://www.accountingtools.com/articles/what-is-the-difference-between-a-journal-and-a-ledger.html.

Bragg, S. (2019, March 20). Financial statement analysis. Retrieved from https://www.accountingtools.com/articles/2017/5/14/financial-statement-analysis.

Cash Basis Accounting vs. Accrual Accounting: Bench
Accounting. (n.d.). Retrieved from
https://bench.co/blog/accounting/cash-vs-accrual-
accounting/.

Cash Flow Statement Template for Excel. (n.d.).
Retrieved from
https://www.vertex42.com/ExcelTemplates/cash-flow-
statement.html.

Chart of accounts. (2019, September 27). Retrieved
from https://en.wikipedia.org/wiki/Chart_of_accounts.

Chen, J. (2019, April 25). Accounting Method. Retrieved
from
https://www.investopedia.com/terms/a/accountingmetho
d.asp.

Chou, L. (2019, June 26). Guide to Financial Statement
Analysis for Beginners. Retrieved from
https://towardsdatascience.com/guide-to-financial-
statement-analysis-for-beginners-835d551b8e29.

Chughtai, B., Norman, A., Julia, Robinson, Parker, J., Shelton, C., & Debitoor, W. (2019, June 11). Small Business Bookkeeping, Accounting & Tax Guide. Retrieved from https://fitsmallbusiness.com/small-business-bookkeeping-accounting-the-ultimate-guide/.

Closing the Books. (n.d.). Retrieved from https://www.accountingtools.com/closing-the-books.

Debits and credits. (2019, October 3). Retrieved from https://en.wikipedia.org/wiki/Debits_and_credits.

Debits and Credits: A Simple, Visual Guide: Bench Accounting. (n.d.). Retrieved from https://bench.co/blog/bookkeeping/debits-credits/.

Debits and Credits: Explanation: AccountingCoach. (n.d.). Retrieved from https://www.accountingcoach.com/debits-and-credits/explanation.

Decker, F. (2019, April 5). How to Keep Accounting Records for a Small Restaurant. Retrieved from https://smallbusiness.chron.com/keep-accounting-records-small-restaurant-56253.html.

Double Entry Accounting Principles vs. Single Entry, Examples. (2019, September 11). Retrieved from https://www.business-case-analysis.com/double-entry-system.html.

Double Entry Bookkeeping in 7 Steps. (n.d.). Retrieved from https://www.beginner-bookkeeping.com/double-entry-bookkeeping.html.

Edunote.info@gmail.com. (2019, October 2). 7 Different Types of Journal Book. Retrieved from https://iedunote.com/types-of-accounting-journal.

Elmblad, S. (2019, May 19). What Is Double Entry Accounting? Retrieved from https://www.thebalance.com/what-is-double-entry-accounting-1293675.

Esajian, P. (2019, September 5). Real Estate Bookkeeping 101. Retrieved from https://www.fortunebuilders.com/real-estate-bookkeeping-managing-finances/.

Financial Accounting. (n.d.). Retrieved from https://courses.lumenlearning.com/sac-finaccounting/chapter/assets-liabilities-and-owners-equity/.

Financial Accounting. (n.d.). Retrieved from https://courses.lumenlearning.com/sac-finaccounting/chapter/preparing-a-trial-balance/.

Financial Accounting. (n.d.). Retrieved from https://courses.lumenlearning.com/sac-finaccounting/chapter/financial-statements/.

Financial statement. (2019, October 6). Retrieved from https://en.wikipedia.org/wiki/Financial_statement.

Financial statement analysis. (2019, August 16). Retrieved from https://en.wikipedia.org/wiki/Financial_statement_analysis.

Financial Statement Preparation: Example: Explanation of Steps. (n.d.). Retrieved from https://www.myaccountingcourse.com/accounting-cycle/financial-statement-preparation.

Financial Statements. (-1, November 30). Retrieved from https://www.inc.com/encyclopedia/financial-statements.html.

Free QuickBooks Tutorials - Learn How To Use QuickBooks. (2016, May 25). Retrieved from https://quickbookstraining.com/tutorials/.

FreshBooks. (n.d.). What is a Ledger in Accounting? Is There a Difference with a Journal and a Ledger? Retrieved from https://www.freshbooks.com/hub/accounting/what-is-a-ledger.

FreshBooks. (n.d.). How to Close the Books: 8 Steps for Small Business Owners. Retrieved from https://www.freshbooks.com/hub/accounting/closing-books.

Good bookkeeping: how to record receipts of transactions. (n.d.). Retrieved from https://www.ionos.com/startupguide/grow-your-business/good-bookkeeping-how-to-record-receipts-of-transactions/.

Grigg, B. A. (2019, October 8). Best Accounting Methods for Small Business: Fundera. Retrieved from https://www.fundera.com/blog/accounting-methods-for-small-business.

How to organize business receipts and paperwork. (2018, November 16). Retrieved from https://amynorthardcpa.com/organize-business-receipts-paperwork/.

Hyre, J., & Conflitti, J. (n.d.). Bookkeeping for Real Estate Investors: RWN Learning Center. Retrieved from https://www.realwealthnetwork.com/topics/bookkeeping/.

Income Statement Template for Excel. (n.d.). Retrieved from https://www.vertex42.com/ExcelTemplates/cash-flow-statement.html.

Ingram, D. (2016, October 26). How to Do Bookkeeping for a Store. Retrieved from https://smallbusiness.chron.com/bookkeeping-store-69569.html.

Investopedia. (2019, September 13). The Difference Between a General Ledger and a General Journal. Retrieved from https://www.investopedia.com/ask/answers/030915/whats-difference-between-general-ledger-and-general-journal.asp.

Irby, L. T. (2019, May 14). The 8 Best Receipt Scanners and Trackers of 2019. Retrieved from https://www.thebalancesmb.com/best-receipt-scanners-and-trackers-4172461.

Kehrer, D. (2019, March 21). The 10 Bookkeeping Basics You Can't Ignore. Retrieved from https://www.score.org/resource/10-bookkeeping-basics-you-cant-ignore.

Kenton, W. (2019, September 12). Financial Statement Analysis. Retrieved from https://www.investopedia.com/terms/f/financial-statement-analysis.asp.

Learn the Basics of Closing Your Books. (n.d.). Retrieved from https://www.bizfilings.com/toolkit/research-topics/finance/basic-accounting/learn-the-basics-of-closing-your-books.

Ledger, General Ledger Role in Accounting Defined and Explained. (2019, September 11). Retrieved from https://www.business-case-analysis.com/ledger.html.

Leonard, K. (2019, March 1). The Differences Between Debit & Credit in Accounting. Retrieved from https://smallbusiness.chron.com/differences-between-debit-credit-accounting-4063.html.

Lewis, M. R. (2019, March 29). How to Understand Debits and Credits. Retrieved from https://m.wikihow.com/Understand-Debits-and-Credits.

Marshall, D. (n.d.). Retrieved from http://www.dwmbeancounter.com/bookkeeping-systems.html.

Murphy, C. B. (2019, October 8). How to Interpret Financial Statements. Retrieved from https://www.investopedia.com/terms/f/financial-statements.asp.

Murray, J. (2019, January 25). A Business Guide to Deducting Legal and Professional Fees. Retrieved from https://www.thebalancesmb.com/deducting-legal-and-professional-fees-for-business-398955.

Nikolakopulos, A. (2017, November 21). Types of Bookkeeping. Retrieved from https://smallbusiness.chron.com/types-bookkeeping-48070.html.

Orange County Trusted Bookkeeper. (n.d.). Retrieved from https://ohanacpb.com/personal-bookkeeping/.

Outsource Services Home. (n.d.). Retrieved from https://www.outsource2india.com/financial/articles/book keeping-systems.asp.

Over 75 FREE QuickBooks Online training tutorials and videos. (n.d.). Retrieved from https://5minutebookkeeping.com/quickbooks-online-tutorials/.

Padhy, B. K. (2019, September 24). Debit vs Credit in Accounting: Top 7 Differences You Must Know! Retrieved from https://www.wallstreetmojo.com/debit-vs-credit-in-accounting/.

Padhy, B. K. (2019, September 24). Journal vs Ledger: Top 9 Must Know Differences (Infographics). Retrieved from https://www.wallstreetmojo.com/journal-vs-ledger/.

Peacock, L. (n.d.). Prevent Tax Troubles by Getting Organized in 2018. Retrieved from https://www.waveapps.com/blog/start-organizing-your-next-years-filing-now.

Peavler, R. (2019, May 4). The Business Owner's Guide to Accounting and Bookkeeping. Retrieved from https://www.thebalancesmb.com/bookkeeping-101-a-beginning-tutorial-392961.

Peavler, R. (2019, July 4). Tips and Guidance for Creating a General Ledger for Your Business. Retrieved from https://www.thebalancesmb.com/constructing-the-general-ledger-for-your-small-business-392998.

Peavler, R. (2019, July 12). You Need to Prepare These Financial Statements at the Cycle's End. Retrieved from https://www.thebalancesmb.com/prepare-the-financial-statements-393008.

Peavler, R. (2019, August 27). Use Horizontal and Vertical Analysis to Determine Financial Performance. Retrieved from https://www.thebalancesmb.com/how-do-you-do-financial-statement-analysis-393235.

Personal & Professional Services. (n.d.). Retrieved from https://rothcocpa.com/industries/personal-professional-services/.

Preparation of Trial Balance: Steps in the Preparation of Trial Balance. (2019, September 4). Retrieved from https://www.toppr.com/guides/principles-and-practice-of-accounting/trial-balance/preparation-of-trial-balance/.

Preparing a Trial Balance for Your Business. (n.d.). Retrieved from https://www.dummies.com/business/accounting/preparing-a-trial-balance-for-your-business/.

Qadeem, A. (2016, June 19). T-Accounts Ledger: Format: Examples. Retrieved from http://www.accountingsheet.com/accounting-cycle/t-accounts/.

QuickBooks. (2019, September 4). Retrieved from https://en.wikipedia.org/wiki/QuickBooks.

QuickBooks Tutorials - Learn How To Use QuickBooks. (n.d.). Retrieved from https://quickbooks.intuit.com/tutorials/.

Rampton, J. (2019, June 24). Complete Guide to Double-Entry Bookkeeping. Retrieved from https://quickbooks.intuit.com/global/resources/bookkeeping/complete-guide-to-double-entry-bookkeeping/.

REIbooks – Bookkeeping Solutions for Real Estate Investors. (n.d.). Retrieved from https://reibooksonline.com/.

Restaurant Accounting 101: How to Manage Your Bookkeeping. (n.d.). Retrieved from https://www.touchbistro.com/blog/restaurant-accounting-101-how-to-manage-your-bookkeeping.

Richards-Gustafson, F. (2017, November 21). How to Open a New Restaurant With Bookkeeping. Retrieved from https://smallbusiness.chron.com/open-new-restaurant-bookkeeping-26151.html.

Roberge, M. (n.d.). Restaurant Bookkeeping 101 - 5 Step Simple Guide. Retrieved from https://www.slcbookkeeping.com/blog/restaurant-bookkeeping-simple-5-step-guide.

Rosenberg, E. (2019, May 24). The 8 Best Accounting Apps for Independent Contractors in 2019. Retrieved from https://www.thebalance.com/best-accounting-apps-for-independent-contractors-4172220.

Singh, J. (2019, September 17). Financial Statement (Examples): Top 4 Types of Financial Statements. Retrieved from https://www.wallstreetmojo.com/financial-statements/.

Staff, I. (-1, November 30). Accounting Methods. Retrieved from https://www.inc.com/encyclopedia/accounting-methods.html.

Staff, M. F. (2016, March 20). What Is a Financial Statement? Retrieved from https://www.fool.com/knowledge-center/financial-statement.aspx.

Staff, W. (n.d.). A Complete Guide to Small Business Tax Season. Retrieved from https://www.waveapps.com/blog/the-complete-guide-to-small-business-tax-season.

Stafford, A. (n.d.). Should Real Estate Investors Be Using Accounting Software? Retrieved from https://www.therealestatecpa.com/blog/bookkeeping-for-real-estate-investors-should-you-be-using-accounting-software.

Dept. of the Treasury, Internal Revenue Service. Starting a business and keeping records, Starting a business and keeping records (1995). Washington, D.C.

Summary: Bookkeeping Basics. (n.d.). Retrieved from https://www.accountingtools.com/summary-bookkeeping-basics.

The General Ledger. (n.d.). Retrieved from https://www.principlesofaccounting.com/chapter-2/the-general-ledger/.

The Ultimate Guide to Real Estate Accounting. (n.d.). Retrieved from https://www.contactually.com/blog/real-estate-accounting.

Tuovila, A. (2019, September 30). Cash Book Definition. Retrieved from https://www.investopedia.com/terms/c/cash-book.asp.

Turner, B., Smith, S., Faircloth, M., & Sharkansky, M. (2019, June 29). The Investor's Guide to Excellent Real Estate Bookkeeping: Blog. Retrieved from https://www.biggerpockets.com/blog/2016-02-17-simple-guide-excellent-bookkeeping-real-estate-investing.

Types of Accounts in Accounting: Assets, Expenses, Liabilities, & More. (2019, July 2). Retrieved from https://www.patriotsoftware.com/accounting/training/blog/types-of-accounts-subaccounts-accounting/.

Understanding Accounting Methods. (n.d.). Retrieved from https://www.dummies.com/business/accounting/understanding-accounting-methods/.

WebstaurantStore. (2019, August 2). Restaurant Accounting Tips. Retrieved from https://www.webstaurantstore.com/article/134/restaurant-accounting-tips.html.

Weltman, B. (2019, June 29). Do I Need A Personal Accountant? Retrieved from https://www.investopedia.com/articles/personal-finance/040115/do-i-need-personal-accountant.asp.

What Are Assets, Liabilities, and Equity?: Bench Accounting. (n.d.). Retrieved from https://bench.co/blog/accounting/assets-liabilities-equity/.

What are the Different Types of Ledgers? (n.d.).
Retrieved from
https://www.accountingcapital.com/books-and-accounts/different-types-of-ledgers

What is a Bookkeeping System? (n.d.). Retrieved from
https://www.topaccountingdegrees.org/faq/what-is-a-bookkeeping-system/.

What Is Double-Entry Accounting?: Complete Small
Business Guide. (2017, November 20). Retrieved from
https://www.patriotsoftware.com/accounting/training/blog/an-overview-of-double-entry-bookkeeping/.

What is financial statement? definition and meaning.
(n.d.). Retrieved from
http://www.businessdictionary.com/definition/financial-statement.html.

What is the difference between a general ledger and
general journal?: AccountingCoach. (n.d.). Retrieved
from https://www.accountingcoach.com/blog/general-ledger-general-journal.

What kind of records should I keep. (n.d.). Retrieved
from https://www.irs.gov/businesses/small-businesses-self-employed/what-kind-of-records-should-i-keep.

Made in the USA
Columbia, SC
23 April 2020